D1623905

Good Guys
Bad Guys

This book is based on Shere Hite's
extensive research in the field of the
emotional and sexual lives of women and
men, which she has been documenting for
fifteen years, plus new research collected by
both authors.

Good Guys Bad Guys

The Hite Guide to Smart Choices

Shere Hite
Kate Colleran

Carroll & Graf Publishers, Inc.
New York

Published by arrangement with Pandora Press.

First published in a different edition by Pandora Press in 1989.

First Carroll & Graf edition 1991

Carrol & Graf Publishers, Inc.
260 Fifth Avenue
New York, NY 10001

Library of Congress Cataloging-in-Publication Data

Hite, Shere.
    [Good guys, bad guys, and other lovers]
    Good guys, bad guys : the Hite guide to smart choices / by Shere
Hite and Kate Colleran. —1st Carroll & Graf ed.
        p.   cm.
    Originally published: Good guys, bad guys, and other lovers.
London : Pandora, c1989.
    ISBN 0-88184-686-4 : $18.95
    1. Love. 2. Interpersonal relations. 3. Mate selection—United
States. I. Colleran, Kate, 1959– . II. Title.
HQ801.H56   1991
646.7′7—dc20   91-4499
                                                             CIP

Text design by Terry McCabe

Manufactured in the United States of America

Contents

Good Guys
Bad Guys

A Critique of Psychobabble

We know you won't believe it but . . . you might find some answers here about what's going on in love . . .

Are women obsessed with love? Common, everyday psychobabble insists that if only women would stop loving "too much" (in effect, be more "like men"), they would be happier and wouldn't have so many "emotional problems." This is demeaning and absurd.

Women's interest in love and personal relationships—so often ridiculed—is important. What women are struggling with is one of the most fundamental issues of our times: how to love, how to restore feeling and emotion to life in a world in which competition and fighting, even war, are too often glorified.

Instead of women loving less, why can't men love more, be more supportive and emotionally involved? If women are forced to relegate love to second or third place in their lives—and become "more male than men"—won't everyone be the loser? A better solution could be for men to be more emotive, more giving, and to take on some of women's traditional characteristics.

Most traditional analyses of love look at relationships mistakenly; books on "women's psychology" tend to accept the situation underlying women's "complaints" (and frequent pain) as inevitable. They coo sweetly that they will help us "cure" our supposed emotional defects, thus implicitly defining women as the only ones who should change. Book after book in the last ten years has described to women how they could change *their* behavior or psyches to solve problems with love. None pointed out that since the culture raises most men with destructive and negative attitudes toward women—and even toward their own emotions—clearly, *this* is what should change. Incredibly, when men's pain and questions about love were documented in *The Hite Report on Male Sexuality,* this aroused cries of "male bashing." Neither that volume nor this is anything of the sort. Instead, they offer a way to open up a new dialogue and make love possible and bring great happiness.

While some people have this happiness at present, the divorce statistics and the pages of women's magazines show clearly that the majority of people do not. Why haven't the "How-Women-Can-Change" books of the last decade improved things? Clearly, the New Woman is not finding love any easier. Why is this? And how can things be improved?

Obviously, problems in relationships have as much to do with men as with women. However, as mentioned, an analysis of men's behavior has been pointedly left out of discussions of "female psychology," almost as if female psychology existed by itself, in a void. (One rarely ever hears the term "male psychology"!) This is strange, since obviously, if men are taught in all kinds of ways that they are superior to women, this surely affects how they behave toward women, even women they truly love. And yet, inequality is rarely remarked on as affecting love; indeed, the inequality of the old emotional contract—what is expected of men versus what is expected of women—is so taken for granted, that it is accepted as "the way things are," "the way things have always been," and "the way things will always be." But things *don't* have to be this way.

There is a certain insulting quality to many of the books that have appeared on women and relationships. They speak to women almost as if we were adolescents in waiting, "desperate for a man" or "desperate" for any new "instruction manual" on our "emotional dysfunction" (or "masochism"!) and ways to "fix ourselves." The direction that these books point is negative. It is time, despite possible labels of "man bashers" and "man haters" (Can you believe it?), to equitably search out and redefine the truth as *women* see it, toward the greater good of more loving relationships.

Creating a New Kind of Love

Underlying love relationships between women and men is a deadweight of outdated assumptions that can destroy, or hopelessly tangle, love. They form what we will call an "emotional contract." This contract consists of intricate psychological patterns that reflect our culture but are often mistakenly referred to as "human nature."

In other words, in the world of relationships, the woman is often expected to do most of the emotional housework: she is expected to nurture the man and take care of his emotional needs, draw him out and listen to him, not be overly critical, and be available with sympathy and understanding. While these are good qualities, study after study shows that women say they give more than they get; woman after woman says that she wishes she could get more emotional understanding from men. However, most men are not brought up to think that this is their role.

What to do about this? Read on! One of the basic questions addressed in this book is how to change the emotional contract in relationships. We also explore and reinterpret how women relate to each other.

Many men are privately anguished over how to define their masculinity, what it means to be a man. The majority feel enormous pressure, anger, and frustration in their lives, but usually focus on women as the cause rather than on the values of society. Although it is often said that younger men are different, they are actually just as likely to be caught up in traditional pressues to "stay in control," to fear "being uncool" or a "sissy." It is, in fact, only individual men of every age—those who have thought more deeply about who they are—who have begun to change and communicate more completely.

Men are not "by their nature" anti-emotional or less expressive, but there has been a built-in contradiction between the so-called "male life-style" and human closeness. The lack of emotionality—or the lack of permission to have any emotion other than anger—is very destructive to men, often leaving them feeling isolated and cynical. Men today are faced with the rather formidable choice of either continuing to live their lives as in the past, seeing emotional life as less important—but feeling torn apart by constantly having to suppress or deny their own needs—creating something new.

Some men are beginning to see how their own welfare is tied up with women's fight to restructure their lives and redesign "femininity." Similarly, a conformist "masculinity" is just as much of a pressure on men as predefined "femininity" is on women. However, many men do not see the relevance to them of the women's movement; they do not see the connection between their own feelings of being trapped and alienated—in their marriages, their jobs, their behavior—and the positive critique of society that the women's movement offers. Many see the women's movement simplistically as "women complaining," "raising a ruckus"—they do not understand that some women and men together are changing their relationships (and the family) to create much more happiness and understanding.

This book offers a new analysis and a new vocabulary for discussing relationships. Just because society has created problems between women and men, this does not mean we need to give up relationships. However, it *is* very important to identify what is really going on, as the dynamics set in motion by the current emotional contract can be harmful to women—and tragic for men. Clarifying what is occurring, pinpointing the hidden patterns that can so damage love (and *people*) is what we are about here. This analysis could save a special love in your life before it gets tangled in the web of the outdated Emotional Contract.

This book is also energizing because as women sharing our personal experiences and feelings with each other, we gain strength and know we are not alone. Fortunately, most of us have women friends we can talk to—but great pressure remains in daily situations to tell people that things are "fine," in our personal lives, no matter what. Many magazines and television shows daily reinforce the psychobabble that is all around us. Frequent comments made to a woman who tries to talk about problems she is having with someone she loves often mimic the prejudices of society; for example, if a woman says her relationship is not going well or is not perfect, it is sometimes said that she must be to blame, i.e. she must be "impossible to live with" or she must be "masochistic" or "neurotic." "Well, why do you get yourself into these situations? Why are you picking the wrong men?"

The stereotype that says a woman is a "masochist" if she stays in a relationship that has some problems belies the reality for most women. Many of us have found working relationships with men we love—relationships that are not perfect, but that are worth continuing. We do not want to give them up, we simply want to reconstruct them in more positive ways.

How do you do this? To be realistic, if you choose to be in a relationship with a man, you are probably dealing with at least some of the problems we dissect in this book— problems that society says do not exist (the only problem is you: you love too much, you are confused, you are selfish, your expectations are too high!). But this is a joke, don't let all this woman blaming hurt you—despite the hundreds of books and magazine articles blasting you for all the relationship problems in the world.

The truth is that you are living in an historic period in which relationships between women and men are going through tremendous change. Throughout the twentieth century, and increasingly now, women are striving to democratize the family and their relationships with men. Too many men have yet to fully comprehend and adjust to the changes. And in fact we too still have many questions, including some of the most forbidden, such as: would it be better to love another woman? or, does one need to be in a couple at all?

This book reverses generations of myths about the wimpy psychology of women. It is a book that could change forever your perception of what is going on in your relationship—a book that will clear up any lingering doubts you have about your right *not* to have a relationship, as well as your right to have one with another woman. It is a book that will give you some advice about the problems between women and men, but it will also offer you choices, not dogma, as to new possibilities for your life, plus celebrating many things women have repeatedly been criticized for.

This analysis and way of seeing things is squarely in the democratic tradition. In fact, women's attempt to create emotional equality in relationship is clearly part of the progressive democratic movement for positive social change that is such a hallmark of U.S. tradition.

It is time to revise relationships so that they are more equal, more fun—happier. And time to understand and change what is really going on—so that love can last.

Shere Hite
Kate Colleran
February 1991

Feelings of Love

Men in Love*

"I fell in love with my wife when I was seventeen. It was exciting. It made life beautiful. It made me feel like Superman."

"This air did breathe her scent and her touch was tattooed on my flesh and her warmth was near. The roses did give off more scents and the magic innocence of youth was everywhere and the world was at peace."

"I felt wonderful. There are no words for it. I went around for weeks and months seeing the world as a place of beauty and hope, rather than ugliness and despair. I spent hours being enchanted by the presence of the woman. Every little nook and cranny of my head was comprehended fully and cherished for the first time in my life."

"I do not fall in love very easily. I am very defensive about my freedom and really fight my feelings when I feel like I may be falling in love. This is something I would so like to change. I want to express it more often than I can now."

* From *The Hite Report On Male Sexuality,* Alfred A. Knopf, 1981.

Women in Love*

"The first time I went to bed with him, I felt as though the world had stopped and I was a shooting star sending out enough light to illuminate the blackest of black holes. Both in bed and out, it was an overpowering sensation and I couldn't get enough of him."

"When I first saw him I felt a lurch, a leap, and then a king of internal sigh, an 'At last. Where have you been for so long?' A deep sense of recognition. It also felt scary as hell. He was like everyone I'd ever been in love with before in some small way and then himself, more so. He is beautiful to look at, astoundingly intelligent, very warm and beautifully sensual (but only in bed, almost never in public), his voice makes my ears feel good and my chest and spine, he has very penetrating eyes, his sense of humor is delightful, he can do or figure out almost anything, and he's maddening, frustrating, infuriating, invigorating, unpredictable, uncontrollable, and nice."

"Both times I have been in love I've known it at once. The usual chatter that goes on in your head—which you more or less think of as yourself—suddenly seems much fainter and smaller, and underneath is something larger, quieter, more sure of itself."

* From the 3rd HR, published as *Women and Love: A Cultural Revolution in Progress*, Alfred A. Knopf, 1987.

"Being in love can give pleasure, even joy, but most of the time it's painful, unreal, and uncertain. It took a long time to learn anything from it, and most of what I learned is that I should avoid it."

"I don't have the same kind of wild passion for him like I did with other men. I sometimes wonder if I should stay in this relationship if I don't have a crazy and passionate feeling towards him. This love isn't 'less,' though, it's just different."

Good Guys
Bad Guys

1

Hidden Emotional Patterns in Relationships

Certain patterns emerge repeatedly as women describe their relationships with men. The feelings that these patterns create have been discussed endlessly in magazines, but their source is rarely, or never, analyzed correctly. This makes dealing with them in our private lives even harder: there is advice coming at us from all directions but rarely does it seem to help or alter our situation. In this chapter, we will dissect and rename the problems in what we call the Emotional Contract.

Here are some examples of the confusing situations women describe experiencing:

"I try to open him up. I want to talk about our relationship, feelings, and problems, develop solutions or compromises. He is quiet, so I have to initiate it and drag it out of him. Sometimes, when he finds it hard to express himself, he withdraws. Without communicating, how can you solve anything?"

"I love him and I know he loves me. I always tell him that he should tell me anything he wants, but he never tells me when he's down or depressed—he says he doesn't want to bother anyone with his problems. But why doesn't he believe that I would love for both of us to share everything with each other?"

One young woman remembers that in her first love affair, she felt anxious and uncertain, but was never quite sure why:

"When I was fifteen, I met Charlie. It was an instant crush with lots of eye contact and flirting. Our first 'date' was arranged by his friends talking to my friends and consisted of him coming over to my house one summer afternoon while my parents were away. We had sex right away. There was absolutely no talking. Afterwards, he got up and stuck his head in a sink full of cold water! I felt I had been initiated, and that I must have done a pretty good job if he was so fired up!

"But as time passed, I started to feel anxious a lot of the time. I never knew what he was feeling or whether I was getting it 'right' or not. I somehow felt that if I could get him to like/love me, the anxiety would go away. I thought I could never relax or look slightly less than perfect or he would leave. I tried to become the perfect girlfriend, a sexy boy-toy, armpiece, adorer. The few times I let the real me peek through I experienced rejection the likes of which had only existed on my 'worst fears' list. I went around in a hazy state of panic all the time."

Another woman, slightly older, describes poignantly her feelings for the man she is involved with:

"Last weekend I saw him. We went boat riding, grocery shopping, and then to his home. He was fixing dinner for me. At this point, he grabbed me and kissed me. I was standing in the dark watching the lightning bugs out the window when he came up behind me and put his arms around me and started caressing me, then turned me around and kissed me a couple of times. Later, when we were cooking dinner, he put his arms around me again and *really* started kissing and caressing me. We were both very aroused. We turned off dinner and had sex. Then we ate dinner and went to bed. . . .

"I asked him the next morning if he had any regrets and he said 'No,' and we sat and drank coffee for an hour. When I left, he kissed me again. That was Sunday morning and now it's Thursday night. I don't know if he's made up his mind that he can't handle being with me . . . or that he *does* care for me and is afraid of that."

And another woman wonders at the psychological health of her ex-boyfriend:

"Oh, he was so interesting. Very cute and animated and alive. I felt all his attention on me whenever we talked, intensely on me. He would notice all the best in me. But soon it started to get different. I was giving affection and attention (in a normal way) and it was very clear that he no longer wanted to show me the same. It was like being punished for doing exactly the thing you were asked to do. Sometimes, in the cab ride home from his house, I would cry. I'd look out at the river and remember the good times and feel like I was in the clutches of Jekyll and Hyde."

Rewriting the Emotional Contract: A New Vocabulary

What do these women have in common? Most say they feel they are giving more emotional support and showing more interest and understanding than they are getting. Why are so many women experiencing this problem? They

want to establish more communicative, happier relationships with the men they love but find this difficult. Why is
this so hard?

Read on, as women pinpoint the *real* dynamics (and
some men epitomize them!) of what is going on just below
the surface of much of this confusing and ambiguous behavior.

i. Emotional Withholding

One of the biggest problems in relationships is a pattern
we call emotional withholding. In this pattern of behavior,
a person erects a "fence" around him or herself, keeping
others at a distance. Men often use emotional withholding
with women to maintain control, without being openly aggressive.

It works like this: after the initial "pursuit" during
which the man acts very interested and attentive, he becomes ambivalent in his behavior, keeping the woman
guessing about his feelings; thus, before she knows it, she
is spending a lot of time trying to figure out what is happening, why things are changing, why the relationship
feels so unsettled. She begins to try harder and harder to
please him in an attempt to regain the original love or at
least the sense of connection. This is a power trip for men
that many are not even aware of using.

Emotional withholding takes several forms. The first in-
volves a question we have all probably asked ourselves at
some point:

"Why won't he talk to me?"

This is widely referred to as a "lack of communication."
This is imprecise; usually what is really going on is that the
woman is trying to get the man to "open up" and talk to
her—it is not a two-way problem. Women say over and

over again that they can share feelings and talk with their women friends in a way that seems foreign to many men. They say that most men don't open up in the same way that women do and, more particularly, don't really listen.

Waiting for a man to open up and talk is frustrating—to say the least. Does what these women say sound familiar?

"His refusal to really share himself with me drives me nuts. He just won't tell me what's going on. I always have to ask—and then the answers are minimal, as if I were offering a prize for the least amount of information he could disclose! You'll never know how many hours I've spent trying to figure out whether he *can't* talk to me or just *won't* talk to me."

"He's often silent for hours when we are alone, but not a nice silence, it's a cold silence which gets on my nerves. I would like him to talk more about feelings, reactions, problems, but he's not interested. He will only talk to me if he sees I'm desperate. . . ."

Why is this happening? Don't men like talking to us? As one woman puts it, "Aren't they interested in what the woman they're sleeping with has to say?"

Some are, yes. But others believe that "real men" don't talk about their feelings; that is for women. They believe men should be rational, logical, and objective. Despite all the discussion of the "New Man," a lot of men still seem to panic when they come face-to-face with an emotion:

"I have extreme problems trying to talk about my feelings. I don't have much feeling about a lot of things. My ex-good friend asked me lots of times about my feelings, especially toward her. I didn't elaborate very much or very easily. She wanted to know what my feelings toward her were. Sometimes she asked me to say good things about her. This was usually when she was down in the dumps."

"Why the hell do you want to talk so much? Anyway, communicating is overrated. I don't like it. I don't want to work that hard, to tell you the truth. Just hang out and shut up, relax. Be a *lady*."

"A woman's questions make me silent."

These wordless situations cause many women to wonder, as the young woman just said: "Is it that he *can't* talk to me or just *won't* talk to me?" While many men still buy the stiff-upper-lip worldview, others may simply not *want* to share themselves. Most men are *still* taught (can you believe it?) to be afraid of looking even remotely "wimpy" and, for many, talking about their feelings comes under this category—even though many are aware of the limitations of being this way. And if they are taught this as children, the unlearning of it takes a great deal of desire and effort:

"My lover complains that I don't talk enough—but she has helped me—by questioning and insisting. I must be afraid that I'll be overcome or lose control of my feelings."

"Men are trained at an early age to disregard any and every emotion, and *be strong*. Not only that, they are supposed to be a cross between John Wayne, the Chase Manhattan Bank, and Hugh Hefner. We are only human, for Christsake."

Many men are even taught that they are not supposed to be "over affected" by falling in love, as this woman describes:

"When he leaned over to me and said, 'I love you,' it was a very big deal for me. When I smiled and tears welled up in my eyes, he said, 'God, you don't have to cry. I only said I loved you, nothing's different, it doesn't mean all that much! Jesus!''

And as this man says:
"Love is a huge word to women, and it doesn't mean that much to men.''

"Is he really listening?"

Another way men typically express emotional withholding is by not listening:

"It is extraordinary to have a conversation with a man where you are pouring out something very important that you may have been terrified to tell him or that you have been rehearsing for a long time in order to be as fair and open as you can, and he just carries on with whatever he is doing. It has always been amazing to me that my boyfriend can sit in a room where I am crying and not even look at me. I can't imagine doing that to him.''

"When we first started seeing each other, he would listen—or I thought he listened; maybe he was just enthralled with my presence! Later I noticed that when I spoke, he would wander out of the room, look preoccupied, or totally neglect to answer me, even when I ended my thought with a question.''

"My friends are genuinely interested in how I feel and what I have to say. We take turns talking and listening. Bill only wants a 'good listener' (and a good lay). Once I start to speak up and express myself, he gets uncomfortable.''

Sometimes women are surprised to find that even though a man seems to be hearing them (at least he *looks* like he is listening), he later has absolutely no recollection of anything that was said.

"I tell him something and later he'll say, 'You never told me that.'"

"He does not hear what I'm saying, he hears what he wants to hear."

One delightful college student remembers a type of non-conversation she had recently with a group of men:

"Don was very kind and loving, but he didn't think that what women had to say was nearly as important as what men had to say. We would be hanging out at parties with his friends and some of mine, and the conversation would go something like this:

GUY 1: Yo, Donny, we nailed 'em. [Making a crude victory gesture and then putting Don into a half nelson.]
GUY 2: Yeah, you didn't save that *too* brilliantly, did you, Don?
GUY 1: Hey, Don, wanna beer? Candy, wanna beer? [Don kisses me on the cheek and asks me if I want a beer as he is walking away. I realize it doesn't matter what I say, I'm going to get a beer whether I want one or not. He assumes I want what he wants.]
GUY 2: Candice, where'd you get that hat? [Tweaking the brim of my hat and pinching my cheek as one would a little baby.]
GUY 3: That's a weird hat. I don't mean weird, I've just

never seen one before. Where'd you get it? [This is said without looking at me, sort of glancing around.]

ME: It's from the store in town that sells hats and gloves, you know . . . [I look at him as I say this, but realize the question was not meant to be answered. Silence . . .]

GUY 1: Hey, Don, you going to the Christmas party?

DON: Yeah, Candy and I are going.

ME: When is that? [No one answers me. I am now beginning to feel like jumping up and down and waving my hands in their faces so they take notice. Hello! H-E-L-L-O!]

GUY 2: I'm taking Melissa.

GUY 1: Melissa Capen?

GUY 2: Yeah . . .

GUY 1: You're kidding! She's so hot . . . listen, I gotta go, I have Professor Valentine in the morning and he's giving us an exam on the fundamentals of constitutional law. . . .

ME: I took that last year. He usually asks you questions on—

GUY 2: Sam told me it's all on the first section of the green text.

ME: Um, listen, I know what he asks—

GUY 1 [to Guy 2]: Really? Is he sure?

ME: Um, I'm trying to tell you—[Small beads of sweat are now forming on my temples and upper lip.]

They all collectively decide that the conversation is over —and it is clear that if they were asked to recollect it later, they probably would not remember I was there."

Does this sound all too familiar? It has happened to most of us, and with "nice" men, too. They *are* often nice men, but their attitudes about women are *not* nice: they assume "for the moment" that women are decorative and that their buddies are what matter.

One woman describes how this experience of not being heard makes her feel:

"When he does this I feel all bound up inside, angry and trapped, as though I'm wearing a mask and I can't get it off. He is looking at me but he doesn't see me. I am speaking coherently, so why can't I be heard?"

The message we get here is that these men are definitely not taking us seriously, and they sure as hell aren't interested in who we really are! They don't pick up on the subjects we initiate. One woman puts it like this:

"Sure, we talk. As long as the subject is something he's interested in. If I want to bring something up that I'm interested in, forget it. I don't even try anymore."

Listen to this man's explanation of this dynamic. Recognize him?

"No, I stopped talking to her much because she was all over me to talk, talk, talk. It's like they get the 'talking disease.' You know, they change after you get them. First they're easy and nice, then the honeymoon's over and they turn into witches who want to talk."

Some men are more aware of what is going on but feel unable to change:

"Lots of times I feel like a robot or Mr. Spock from *Star Trek,* not able to show my feelings when they seem appropriate. Because of this I find it very difficult to take a lot of situations seriously and I attempt to make light of them or dull their importance. I can't hardly ever show my true feelings.''

When your remarks are met by silence

Women say that they are often greeted by silence when they offer their comments, even in small talk. We heard the following "conversation" on the street:

WOMAN: That's a pretty dog.
MAN: [no response]
WOMAN: Well, it's got a pretty coat.
MAN: [Silence]

Women trying to live with men who are silent, or men who talk as little as they can and reveal even less, have a frustrating time of it. Under these circumstances, a woman may start to feel panicky and emotionally uncertain, thinking, "He loved/wanted me in the beginning—what happened?" Then she may think to herself, reasoning, *"He* is so different now from the way he was in the beginning. Who is the 'real' man: the one I first met or this one? It must be the first one I met, he's only behaving this way because there is some problem. Let me help him figure it out. As one who loves him, I shouldn't desert him just because things are difficult for the moment . . . We can work it out, together!"

But if a woman tells the man, "You are behaving so differently, you're almost hostile—why?" she may very well hear, "I haven't done anything wrong! I haven't even said anything!" Exactly.

This insecure feeling on the woman's part is a supremely logical response to a very real situation; that is, a relationship in which a man is withholding himself. This is not a "lack of communication" but—to name it more precisely

—a *denial* to the other person of real emotional expression. The man is refusing to share himself on a deeper level.

Sometimes, when women try to talk about this emotional distance with a man he may turn around and say, "Listen, get off my back. Your need for more communication is not realistic, it is an unreasonable expectation, some unresolved thing." But women's desire for more communication is not a neurosis! It *is* something unresolved, an unresolved "male" problem in our society—a society which discourages men from "talking like women do."

While so many books claim that the problems in communication between women and men spring from women having "Freudian" neuroses ("masochism" and "insecurity"), in fact these are perfectly reasonable responses to the situation. Furthermore, women say here that what is often described as their "demanding" and "complaining" nature is actually one of the few responses possible to emotional withholding by men. This barrier to closeness is something most women passionately wish men would change.

ii. Psychological Aggression

"Why is he so ambivalent?"

Another form of control some men use is an ambivalence that many women describe in the men they know. They say this ambivalence on the part of men often makes them ask themselves, If he loves me, then why is he so emotionally distant one day, so warm the next?

In this form of withholding, a man typically expects the woman to always be there with her love, unwavering, but he himself offers love erratically—just enough to keep her involved. Often, he will say he is "confused" or "can't make up his mind."

One woman recounts the "fun" experience she had during a so-called relationship with a man who kept stringing her along, offering love but never really clarifying his feelings for her:

"He told me he was dating someone who was nice but not exciting. He said 'It just wasn't there' with her. I knew what he meant because I had felt like that before. Although we were very attracted to each other, we agreed it would be better not to sleep together until he was free. He said it would be a matter of a few weeks. But when he was next in town, we spent the night together anyway. Then I didn't hear from him for ten days. Rude. When he eventually called with some story, I told him no one could sleep with me and then not even bother to call. He apologized and I accepted it, because our night together had been *so* wonderful. And I just *knew* how much he felt for me—at least I thought I did.

"We slept together whenever we got the chance after that, but it wasn't just a sexual thing. We even went away for a romantic weekend. He always said wonderful, romantic things to me, but the next day he would shuffle around and say he was still 'confused,' 'unsure.' It was devastating. And each time it happened, I became more distrustful and resentful. But I was hooked.

"I started to fall really heavily. I truly believed that he had fallen for me too, but, when push came to shove, he always wanted to 'do the right thing'—that meant 'not hurting' this other woman and 'not hurting' me, either.

"Each time he came to stay, I thought, This is it. Our night will be so great that he'll wake up and say to himself, What am I doing? Let me take the risk and find what I've always wanted here!

"Then one day he called me and said that we couldn't

see each other again 'in that way.' There was no way I wanted to be 'friends,' so I said I never wanted to see him again.

"A few months later, he called to tell me he had finally finished his relationship with the other woman. I told him to fuck off. I found out much later he was only 'free' for about twenty-four hours! He's still seeing her today."

Guessing games: the not-knowing

"What drives me crazy in a relationship is the not know-ing . . . not knowing if he really loves me, if he wants to marry me eventually, if he is just going along to see if we get along ok before he brings it up, or is he just taking me for a joyride for however long it lasts?"

Who, when they listen to this woman, doesn't empathize —hearing either herself or other women she has known? How many hours have most of us spent trying to figure out what is going on in a man's mind?

That vague, uneasy state of not knowing, the constant wondering what is going on, grows out of many men's pattern of withholding emotion and information from women. It is difficult to face the fact that withholding is a form of power and control commonly used by some men (including those we love). It is painful to realize that some-one could actually want to keep us in line by giving just enough crumbs to keep us hanging on but not enough to make a relationship flourish.

At first, the suspense of not knowing in romance can be exciting, but after a few dates (particularly after the first sexual encounter) what some men may think is sexy, devil-may-care behavior quickly comes to infuse a relationship with insecurity, fear, and distrust:

"That first-he-acts-as-though-he's-crazy-about-you-and-then-he-doesn't-even-call act, no matter how many times it happens to you, never seems to get easier."

Not explaining changes in behavior can also be a form of control some men use:

"I'm wild about him, but there's a feeling of sadness in me all the time. We used to be wild about *each other*. In the last year, though, he has withheld sex from me, and I don't understand it. It's like he's doing this for a reason, but he won't tell me what it is."

One woman describes how she tried to deal with this not knowing by becoming so focused on the man's interests that she completely neglected her own:

"When J. J. said he would be in town in a week we planned to go out one night, and so I rearranged my life to meet him. He didn't turn up and my whole week was wrecked. There I was, a responsible woman, and I was willing to juggle everything to accommodate him because I was so insecure about how he felt about me."

And a charming young musician in school describes her experience with what has to be one of the vaguest relationships on record:

"I had just gone to my first football game in college, and having been used to dating city boys with small physiques and a penchant for looking as sick as they could in mimicry of their rock star idols, I was absolutely paralyzed with fascination at the hunks I saw there. They swore a lot and hung out with each other, and laughed at jokes and phrases I didn't understand that I had a sneaking suspicion were at my expense. But all I wanted was for Al to fall for me.

"One night my friend and I went to a frat party where a lot of 'animal' noises and loud music were emanating from the windows. We went downstairs for a beer. I soon learned that the most important thing to do was to look like you knew where you were going and what you were going there for. God forbid you should look vulnerable or confused.

"So I stood there and pretended to be talking to my friends about incredibly important, fascinating things and brilliant jokes, and they did the same. But we were really waiting for 'them' to notice us.

"Then I was jabbed in the ribs by a not-so-popular-with-the-guys-but-wished-she-were senior who whispered in my ear: 'There's Al.'

"He loomed in the doorway like a Mack truck, power personified. And he knew it. He had a cut on his cheek from the hockey game, wore an old plaid shirt, jeans that hung around his hips over a tiny butt, and a broad grin on his face. He was huge, male to the 'nth' degree, totally involved with his friends and Totally Unavailable.

"Nevertheless, Al and I started to have a sporadic sexual relationship. The night 'it' first happened was at another party after a game. The whole basement floor was drenched in about four inches of warm beer. The 'men' were doing something called the 'beer slide' (very *Animal House*), where they took a running leap at the floor and slid through the beer to the other side of the room. I fleetingly wondered whether this was what college was all about.

"Finally, only the girls with actual boyfriends at the fraternity were still there, so I started to leave. I suppose it may have been stupid and naive to stay that late, but I was having so much fun.

"When he saw me getting my coat, Al shouted across

the room, 'Yo, Susie, stay!' He walked over to me with a smile on his face and picked me up. Across his shoulder. Like a caveman. He carried me upstairs to his room. As he walked in carrying me (giggling) over his shoulder, his roommate looked up and saw us. There were no words spoken, only broad smiles and a punching-of-the-air gesture meant to symbolize victory. The roommate left.

"We went into bunk beds for an episode that lasted approximately ten seconds. It remains the single most unsatisfying physical encounter I have ever had. It was so awful physically, but having done it was like a badge of honor, like being admitted to an exclusive club. I suppose it was kind of silly to want to belong, but even so, he shouldn't have been the way he was afterwards. We went back down to the party and acted as though nothing had happened. Can you believe this was my role model for relationships?

"For the following weeks, nothing happened either. There were no phone calls, some flirting at parties, some (many) parties when he didn't even talk to me at all. Then, one night, we went back to his room and actually 'made love.' He told me I was beautiful, and we had the best time. Now I was on top of the world. He then invited me to his parents' house for the weekend. We got very drunk and had sex in a playing field in the dark with a transistor radio playing Bruce Springsteen. Then we returned to school. Again, nothing—no words.

"By spring break, we met up at a party. We drank, had fun with friends, and went to the beach. I wrote his name in the sand. He pulled my chair next to his (I was on it!) and asked me how I felt about him. It was that I'm-not-going-to-tell-you-how-I-feel-first stuff.

"I wondered why he couldn't tell me first. I talked around my real feelings, not using the word 'love,' which is what I really, really felt. It was obvious that to get this man and keep him, I couldn't say how I really felt, had to act aloof. I wanted desperately to know what he was feeling, wanted so much for it to be love, but I felt it was safer to keep him guessing, just as he kept me guessing.

"He uttered something vague and then he fucked me. I never knew what to make of it. I still don't. I never saw him again. It was all so confusing, the whole thing. Years have passed and I've never quite gotten over Al."

iii. Double Messages—Giving Love and Taking It Back

The double message is another common but unnamed pattern that has become visible as women talk about their relationships. Many men continually send out conflicting signals, as these women explain:

"We were having a quick dinner out. But it got later and later and I said, 'Darling, do you want to go on home and do your work?' (he does desktop publishing). After a silence he said, 'Oh, no,' but with a tone of voice that meant, 'yes'. I then said, 'Really, it's okay, I know you have a lot to do, I understand.' He sat immobile, like a martyr. Did he *really* prefer to be with me? I immediately became preoccupied with whether or not I was pressuring him. Now, why couldn't he just have told me how he really felt? It's so damned unclear."

"I sat across from him in a restaurant last week and he said so many great things to me, it really bowled me over. He even looked like he was crazy for me. But then I met a friend of his yesterday and he said he had gone on vacation to Maine, just like that. Why didn't he tell me he was going? Now I'm obsessed with this trip and what he's doing. If he could just have been less sweet to me and less interested, I wouldn't have gotten so excited."

"He did ask me once to marry him, but then he went out with my friend. He says he loves me and I shouldn't take a one-time fling with her so seriously. Am I living in a fantasy? What does he really want? To me, what he did really says something."

"We were having a nice date. I was wearing a long skirt which was one of his favorites, and he told me I 'looked fantastic.' Then he got up to go to the men's room and he didn't come back for *twenty minutes.* Finally, feeling humiliated and embarrassed, I went downstairs and found him talking to a waitress in a miniskirt. He looked bashful, like he had been 'caught,' and then came upstairs. He said, as if nothing was wrong, 'What a nice girl, and so attractive. Great legs' and then he leaned over and kissed me on the cheek and said, 'I love you, cutie. You look about twelve years old tonight, really adorable.' I'm twenty-six . . . I felt horrible."

How would one react logically to these mixed signals? Women who love men who behave in this way legitimately feel insecure (or irritable): the reality is that their position is unclear. All women are not irrationally "in need of reassurance"; too many men, whether they mean to or not, keep women guessing through their own inner confusion and lack of straightforward messages and actions.

The logical progress of events in a situation like this is: first, the man displays very desirous behavior; the woman responds; the man begins to act ambivalent; the woman tries to figure it out; he denies that there is a problem; she starts to question her own perceptions. Whose "reality" is correct? If she pursues it to try and find out, still feeling uncertain, he may accuse her of "nagging," or call her "neurotic" and "insecure."

Although we can see *logically* that these subtle double messages are the cause of our uneasiness, many of us in this situation hear a small, inner voice that says, "He must be a little bit right. I *am* very insecure. Maybe I *am* hysterical and emotionally dependent! I had better change or I will drive him away. I must stop clinging and become less self-ish, try harder to be more of what he wants me to be." The awful part of this last thought is that we have denied the man's part in this setup—after all, he *did* have something to do with the situation! The result of this collective blaming of self is the plethora of books indicating that women need to "lighten up." Thus, the cycle is kept in motion.

After all this, it's no wonder that hundreds of women every day grab at anything that will provide temporary relief from the frustration and worry: cigarettes, food, whatever. A woman trying to have a relationship with a man is often thrown into a state of anxiety and ends up spending an inordinate amount of time trying to decipher his behavior. This can be nerve-wracking and debilitating. How can you maintain healthy attitudes and self-esteem under these circumstances?

Women deserve more direct communication from men. Why play games?

"Why do I feel lonely and insecure, even when he's telling me he loves me?"

It is remarkable how many women say they have felt that even while a man is telling them he loves them, he is also telling them (indirectly) what is wrong with them.

One woman remembers a particularly infuriating event in her life:

"After the first night we had sex, Eddie put his arms around me, sort of feeling my waist and hips. Then he walked away and sat down. I was feeling so good; I hadn't had any sex for about nine months and his touch had felt exquisite. I really liked him. He was unusual and odd and funny. He then asked me if I was the 'weight that I wanted to be.' I was a little taken aback but said, 'Yes.' He just said, 'Oh,' and walked into the bathroom.

"I sat there feeling devastated. I had just shared my bed with this man, and he was already judging my body, giving no appreciation or reassurance. When he came out, I asked him what this was all about. He said, 'Well, you could lose a few.' When he saw my face fall, he said, 'Don't look so upset. After all, you did ask.' 'Oh,' I thought, 'I see. It was *my* fault. I wasn't perfect and it was *my* problem if I couldn't face the truth. Because we had slept together he apparently owned my body and was well within his rights to criticize it. And if the information bothered me so much, then I only had myself to blame because I *had* asked.' "

Many women live in the midst of other forms of ambiguity:

"Sometimes he seems to love me and like me, other times he doesn't, or he acts cold and distracted. He refuses to talk about our future, even though we have been going out for almost a year and a half. He just changes the subject if I bring it up. I really like him, so I'll try to stick it out. But I feel out of touch and out of control a lot of the time."

"The problem is that first he says he's vulnerable and in love, then later he denies it or doesn't act like it, acts cold. I ask myself, 'Is the goal this man at any cost?' It's almost as if someone is egging me on into the deep end of the pool, but when I get there (with my emotions) and really fall in love, trust him, he says, 'What? Why me?' "

"He says he loves me but he is so changeable, making and breaking dates at the last minute, things like that. So I'm doing something that I really feel pretty ashamed about. I call his apartment to see if he's home when he says he'll be. If he doesn't answer, I go to the club we usually go to and pretend I am out for the evening with other friends, but I'm really just seeing if he's there. If he's not, I look for his friends and try to find out (surreptitiously) where he is and what he's doing. On the other hand, if he's home when I call, I just hang up and tell myself I shouldn't be so childish."

Do these men love these women? Maybe yes, maybe no. Do the men themselves know? And if they don't, is it right to play with someone else's emotions until they figure it out? Men's confusion, withholding of information, and double messages can lead to our spending huge amounts of time wondering what the hell they feel, who the hell they are, trying to figure it all out.

So, even if men do or say contradictory things, they can't be irrational, can they? They must know which one they mean, mustn't they? We must be the ones who can't "get with the program," right? Looking at the dynamics in this way it is amazing to think of women so often being labeled "irrational"!

iv. Basic Assumptions of the Emotional Contract

Men as "stars"

"When I was three or four, my mother was already teaching me to *see* dust and other people's feelings. ('Don't bother your father, he's tired.')"

"Although I find that I'm funny, sarcastic, and energetic when in mixed groups, 'the life of the party'—when my boyfriend's there, boom. I'm very quiet. Almost like I shouldn't steal his 'spotlight.' "

We have heard a lot about the New Man, but how many of us have *genuinely* equal relationships?

"I guess on paper you would say we were equal, being married and both earning a salary. But that's a load of crap in reality. Any big decisions, including ones that directly affect me, are mostly his."

"We live in a real small apartment (one room) on a noisy street. He works nights so he has to get enough rest what with the traffic sounds and all. I try to be real careful about it, I'm always worrying about his rest—I unplug the phone and I don't watch TV. But when I've put in a twelve hour day he doesn't think twice about getting me up for a little sex whenever he feels horny. If I don't act real happy to be woken up (if I seem annoyed), he gets pissed off and sulks. It's sort of like his schedule and needs are the first thing we *both* should think about and mine are second."

"If I was on the phone to one of my customers, he would want me to drop the customer so I could talk to him. If I was in a meeting, he would leave messages for me. I had a territory with several hundred customers and I had to spend a lot of time in the field. If he called me when I was out, when I returned his call he would ask me where I'd been, who I was with, etc. . . . I felt like a little kid checking in with my dad."

So many men seem to assume that their opinions and ideas are more important than women's, and that their own needs come first. Of course, many so-called New Men would deny this, express surprise at the accusation, or react more angrily.

But the fact is, most women are *still* in the unfair position of having to struggle against men's assumptions that *their* view of reality is the *correct* view—no dialogue necessary:

"What we do is always his decision—whether we go out to eat in the first place, then whether we have dinner alone or with friends, when he calls me, if we have sex, and so on."

One woman feels her relationship slipping away because of this:

"At first it was just like in the movies. We couldn't get enough of each other, body and mind. Then I started to want to talk more, to work things out before they got to be really big problems, like: how often we saw his mother, what we spent on credit cards, the way he ignored me at parties. But he always changed the subject as soon as I started to explain. He would say he was going to go work out, hang out with some friends, go fishing. It always happened to be right after I had brought something up. It got to the point where I would sit in the window of our apartment and watch him drive away and look down at the ring on my finger and wonder, 'What is happening? How did it get like this? It wasn't always like this, was it?'"

This problem has existed for a long time. Most of our homes were controlled, either overtly or covertly, by the "head" of the household (our father). Boys who grow up in families like this tend to perpetuate this belief system in their own lives, forming the same patterns with women they love/live with. These leftover assumptions are what women today find themselves trying so hard to highlight and change.

Many women tell poignant stories of this dynamic in their own childhoods:

"When I got home from school in the afternoons, my mother and I would talk about what had happened that day, fix something in the kitchen, hang out. When we heard the car pull in the drive, that meant my father was home from work, and the tone would change. My mother would become distant, and prepare to greet him. The rest of the evening she and I would remain distant, not really talking to one another, as if somehow that would be intrusive to him, would offend his sense of being given most of the attention. It was never anything explicit, just a feeling in the air."

"I learned from my mother that the proper attitude toward my father was to defer to him and give his opinions the most time and attention."

"My father would criticize me for everything, from little things to big things. When he decided that a particular night was going to be one where he 'taught us something,' my sister and I knew we were in for a long one. We weren't allowed to express ourselves at all, just had to sit there and take the criticism and the endless lectures and the insistence that if we didn't live life in *his* way, we would end up where we belonged, 'hussies on the street corner.' He always managed to mention sex and the 'looseness of women.' If I ever tried to talk back to him, or just simply express my own point of view, I would get blasted from here to the moon. I learned it wasn't worth it, but I still tried now and then. I just couldn't stand the pain of my own silence."

Do men define reality?

Again and again, women describe men's assumptions that they are right, have the right to criticize women's opinions and actions but not to be criticized themselves:

"When we have a disagreement, he belittles me into being quiet. He has this need to always be right, which certainly does not solve anything."

"As usual, he interrupted me on the phone to tell me I was crazy and stupid to suggest what I was saying."

When you are in this kind of relationship you may find that you apologize when you don't really want to, just to keep the peace. This practice is painful and is usually very destructive to you in the long run. Having to deny your feelings and who you are—to ignore how you *really* feel— is always very damaging on a long-term basis.

"I was wearing a lovely summer dress that he hadn't seen before. It had embroidery on the front, with *tiny* little holes in the stitching. It was backless so I couldn't wear a bra with it. He said, 'Jesus, I think I can see your nipples through those holes. I can't believe you would wear that!' I said I thought he would like it, that no one else could see. I thought it was romantic. He was furious, standing there in the tightest pants on record. When we got home, I had to spend an hour apologizing for embarrassing him in pub- lic and for wearing such a stupid fucking dress."

Women as co-stars

"Generally, men live their lives as though they were starring in them . . . many men will never take the time and effort to find out what's inside their mates. Co-stars."

As that 'star', a man will set the agenda of emotional "reality" in the relationship—sometimes psychologically bullying a woman into "accepting" his terms even though she may not agree with them. But if she wants him, she may have to accept his definition of things ("reality") thus damaging herself by internalizing the idea that *her* perception of reality is slightly "crazy," "neurotic," or at least "wrong."

These powerful unacknowledged dynamics can have a pernicious effect on a relationship, as one woman describes:

"Ed believed that all our problems were my fault, and was so convincing that my own perception of what was really going on became distorted. As the relationship 'grew,' I became trapped in a downward spiral, unable to express my doubts or problems—I censored *myself* after a while, assuming the problems were mine and I should 'work on myself' to figure them out."

By acting as if their needs are more important than ours, that their version of reality is real and ours is not, then telling us when we try to point this out that we are "whining" and "insecure," some men are practicing a form of doublespeak and psychological abuse. They are illogically putting us down for our very logical reaction to tyranny.

In relationships, there should be mutual discussion of situations to arrive at a consensus. But many men are not yet ready to really "hear" women to this extent; they assume without really thinking that their view of reality and the relationship is right.

v. Emotional Battering

Bitchy comments from men to women

"He's always criticizing me. Then he says, 'What's the matter? Can't you take it?' "

Women's daily lives are "enhanced" by the sort of casual criticism this woman describes:

"When I didn't wash my hair one evening, the first thing my boyfriend said to me was, 'Oh, didn't you wash your hair today, hon? Well, it looks alright,' in this kind of fake sweet voice. Or another time I wore sexy lingerie I thought he'd like and he said, 'What's the matter, couldn't you afford more expensive stuff? That looks kind of sleazy.' Or the other day when I went out to a movie with my friends, he found out when it was over, decided what time I 'should' get home, then yelled at me for 'hanging out with the girls all night' while he waited. I knew he was being ridiculous (I waited for him a lot) but I did hesitate about going out with my friends again."

This kind of pattern works like intimidation. The next time it happens, we try to modify our behavior, as this woman describes:

"With this guy I starve myself to look thin, rush home from work to make the house look really welcoming, try everything to make him happy so he won't complain. My reward? Last week he said to me, 'You're so perfect,

you're becoming a real drag. Why can't you be more feminine?' Now I'm trying to figure out how to do *that*."

Sometimes if a woman then complains or asks for clarifi-
cation, the man will say, 'Oh, why are you so sensitive? I
was only teasing you!' (Sometimes adding, 'you know I
love you'). But these kinds of sideswipes and unproductive
criticisms are similar to the double messages women talked
about earlier; women have several layers of meaning to
deal with which leads them to become preoccupied with
trying to figure out what these layers are. They hope that
straightening out the "problems" will lead to the original
love in the relationship returning.

The "fun" of language

Some forms of criticism are so standard that they are
built into the language—you know, those good old clichés
that are reserved just for women! Have you ever been told
you are:

> pushy, demanding, complaining, neurotic, hysterical,
> screaming, irrational, needy of reassurance, overemo-
> tional, too sensitive, babyish, crazy, in need of help, er-
> ratic, moody, at it again, nagging, or difficult?

And how often do you hear men called any of these
things?

Unfortunately, many men who love women still plug
into this kind of language when they are irritated or upset;
these words just creep into the conversation. They may
also be used by strangers, "just in passing." To challenge
them, under the circumstances, would seem to be overreacting. But it would be very understandable if a woman
did react angrily at being called names that, given their

history and meaning, have for generations been used to put women down or "keep them in their place."

While we may shrug off these words in general, when someone we love starts using them, it is difficult not to be shaken by self-doubt. If we then turn to that same person for reassurance, we stand a good chance of being put down for asking. This becomes a self-fulfilling trap, for there is no end to what we can blame ourselves for when someone we love is pointing out what is wrong with us.

Shut up by stereotypes?

Lots of women describe the names men call them:

"When my friends and I try to make plans with our boyfriends, ask when they will be home and so on (we all have a summer house together), they call us things like 'nags,' 'policewomen,' 'ball-and-chains.' One guy, when he was out with his friends (with his girlfriend waiting at home) even called her 'The Terminator,' like the movie title."

These labels can either be enraging or hysterically funny, depending on one's mood. It goes without saying that very few women *want* to act as killjoys or be labeled as such. Women make "rules" or ask questions when the men in their lives show little consideration: the "rules" and questions are women's attempt to make the relationship work by drawing the line *somewhere,* before they get so angry that they just walk out.

The cowardly critic

Another form of hostility is more insidious; it is heavily veiled criticism that makes you end up thinking you are crazy. And the critic supports that belief, saying, "I treat you so well—you must be paranoid."

This pattern of veiled criticism, being attacked indirectly, was the thread running through one woman's long relationship:

"After going out with Larry for about nine months—lots of parties and all—I started to need more closeness. There was virtually no intimacy, we were just the party pair. I began trying to be more romantic, to cook great dinners, have whole evenings when we stayed in bed, spent time together. But it was like swimming upstream. I tried really hard, but it got lonelier and lonelier. On the other hand he was always around, wanting to go out with me, so I thought he must care.

"Eventually I started crying every morning, *every day,* because our perfunctory sex the night before left me feeling so hollow. I tried to tell him this but we would fight again because he hated me crying. He called my tears 'morning sickness.'

"I decided to make one last stab at getting things to be different. A couple from France were visiting and we planned a big party (Larry is French). I bought a terrific new outfit, did myself up, and then made my entrance. He looked me up and down and said nothing. But when the Frenchwoman walked out of her bedroom to join us, he said, watching her every move, 'She looks incredible! Frenchwomen have such style, don't you think?' (I am *not* French.) He must have known how this made me feel, the brilliant sadist that he was. What a great way to keep me in my place."

Being constantly put down, *especially* indirectly, plus having your thoughts or feelings ignored or flatly dismissed as "ridiculous" by the one who says he loves you, is confusing to say the least. How on earth do you reconcile feelings of "love" with this kind of behavior?

Criticism is normal, of course. Throughout any relationship, people who love one another criticize each other—hopefully with tenderness and a constructive aim. But what women here are describing is different: a pattern of constant, indirect criticism, being diminished as part of a daily routine, which amounts to emotional abuse. We have seen the clichéd insults that are such a part of everyday language—language which men frequently accept as OK. This problem is compounded by the fact that, since society tells men that they are the natural "stars" of relationships, they often assume they have the right to "set the standards" for our behavior and inform us when we do not meet these standards—to tell us what is "wrong" with us.

When this emotional battering becomes a way of life, it is difficult to make the man stop and realize that his assumptions and premises are bigoted—and so persuade him to rethink and change them before the relationship is ruined.

Sabotage

Some women say their relationships contain incidents in which their partner forgets things that matter or seems to trivialize them:

"My husband would make my life harder, but never in ways I could really 'catch him.' For example, I was hosting a barbecue for about forty of my colleagues—it was an important occasion for me. While I was out of the house, one colleague phoned to inquire whether he still needed to bring his extra skewers—my husband said no, leaving me without an adequate number to serve everybody. To this day, I don't know whether he really didn't know I was short (but why didn't he tell the man to bring them anyway, if he wasn't sure?) or if it was some subtle way of getting back at me for being so 'overly preoccupied' with 'fussing' over my 'little party.' "

"It was my twenty-ninth birthday and I was feeling good. I went home from work and got a bouquet from my mom and calls from friends, but nothing from my boyfriend. I was disappointed, but I guessed he was getting ready or out getting me something.

"We had planned to meet at my favorite restaurant, my boyfriend and about ten other friends. He didn't really like my friends (and they didn't like him much either), but I thought it would probably be OK just for tonight, since it was my birthday.

"I got to the restaurant early and waited at the bar. My friends started arriving, with tulips and little presents. It was so sweet, and I felt so happy to be cared for.

"Then he walked in, no smile or anything. He thrust an old plastic bag into my hand. I opened it and inside there was a toy meant for four year olds. You pull a little string and it tells you how to cross the street or say thank you. I couldn't believe it. I looked up at my best friend and saw her seething. This was not funny, it was like him saying, 'I'll give you what I want, when I want, and if you don't like it, tough.' It was like, 'Let's see how much humiliation you can take and still be gracious.'

"Throughout dinner he ignored me or was rude and insulting, so the whole table was silenced. More friends arrived, and at this point I was embarrassed at how nice they were being to me because it showed how lousy *he* was being. I was so ashamed.

"Finally, I had to get up from the table because I felt unable to hold back my tears. I was so hurt. But I dared not let him see, because God knows what he would have said then. My girlfriend laid into him, and when he refused to chip in for my meal like everyone else had, they all left. They couldn't stand it anymore, and I didn't blame them.

"Then outside he started in on me, yelling at me about my friends, what was wrong with them, how shitty I was to be so upset, what's the matter with me, blah, blah, blah. I just stood there and cried. How could I explain to him when he was so removed from what had actually happened?

"In the end, I just kept saying over and over, 'It's my birthday, how could you do this? It's my birthday . . .' and jumped in a cab. P.S. We broke up after that night."

This sabotage leaves women feeling very lonely in their relationships—*more* lonely than if they were on their own:

"During the last relationship I had with a man I spent moments so lonely I sometimes wondered if everyone else had disappeared off the face of the earth."

"I'm so glad to have finally divorced him and started my life again because I felt so incredibly alone when we were married. Isolated. Ignored. Now I can give more attention to my son and have fun and experience life without the fear that I'm going to be 'iced'—my husband was a genius at being so cold when he didn't want to talk that you could swear you were in Siberia."

vi. Emotional Housework*

We have seen that feelings of "insecurity" or doubt women may have are usually a logical reaction to a complex interaction: if a man insists on withholding his feelings, this puts a burden on the woman to "try to under-

---

* Term originated by Gudula Lorez.

stand" and open up communication, to do most of the "emotional housework." By doing this emotional work, women are making relationships possible. How ironic, then, to put women down for this! How ridiculous to berate women for being "too demanding" and "always wanting to talk."

There is another irony here: while women are labeled as needing to talk and communicate more, most men are already getting this kind of attention from women, so they do not have to ask for it (or be seen to need it). Isn't it interesting to note that most men do not turn to other men to fulfill their emotional needs? In *The Hite Report on Male Sexuality* the great majority of married men said their best friends were their wives. However, in *Women and Love* most married women, although they generally said they loved their husbands, also said that if *they* want to talk, they turn to their best friends: women.

In short, the reality behind many of these situations is not that women are neurotic Freudian shadow women who live their lives in agonies of insecurity. The truth is that the dynamics many men set in motion make it necessary for women to question what is going on: why the man is saying the things he says and whether he really wants to be in the relationship anyway. It is a pity that so many of the intricate feelings we happily share with other women are blocked by men; we cannot talk as easily with them because they feel uncomfortable.

What women are saying is that they wish men would drop their outdated ideas about themselves and about women, stop being afraid of being seen as "weak," and start empathizing rather than competing with women. Turn over a new leaf and learn to love with emotional equality—without fear.

vii. Emotional Violence: A Definition

Living in an emotionally aggressive atmosphere

Much of what results from these patterns—if repeated or carried to an extreme—constitutes what we term emotional violence—"E.V." The attitudes surrounding E.V. are built into behavior toward women and these ways of speaking to women, form the background against which most relationships are acted out. This frame of reference can create so much tension, defensiveness, and discomfort that many single women even try to avoid getting involved in new relationships. Thus it is no surprise that even men who love women can use hideous stereotypes in their relationships with women without fully realizing what they are doing.

This not so subtle aggression and harassment is so prevalent and all pervasive in our society that it is generally accepted as "normality"; we are told it is "human nature," "men are like that," and that words like "harassment," "battery," and "aggression" are "exaggerations."

E.V. is a large-scale social problem, not a biologically determined "way things are." The dynamics in which women are seen as "masochists" who love pain or "bitches" who are "disloyal" and won't "stand by their man"—these are not reality, they are hostile caricatures reflecting women's inequality in society. But we are told that women and men become equal in love. Thus, the problems caused by women's second-class status are swept under the carpet, called "women's problems," and left for women to solve—alone. E.V. is covered up with tranquilizers and bad advice on how to "live with it" or "hurry up and change to get/keep your man."

This nasty Freudian-descended view of women as deserving their second-class status has suffused much of twentieth century art, literature, and politics. In this book, we are breaking with that tradition and presenting a new analysis of what is going on.

However, if one remembers that it was only ten years ago that statistics on physical battering were exposed (and it has been shown that over 85 percent of cases of spouse abuse are carried out by men), it is obvious that a climate of emotional abuse would be more prevalent than its extreme form, physical abuse. Some examples of E.V.—which we will certainly see more of in this book—are as follows:

"Christ, it's way overdone this thing about men abusing women. Women are getting away with murder. They get everything they want and then if we complain later we're assholes."

"Women just need to sound off. The greatest people alive were men, including J.C. himself. No woman has yet lived and been great enough to be the Daughter of God. Print it."

"If they didn't act so childish, I wouldn't think of them as children. Women in positions of power in big business, politics, education, is a crock. It's just another example of the quota system making for reverse discrimination. If men weren't so superior, they wouldn't have attained all the superior status that they have! I mean, it's logical."

"Women overreact to this imagined oppression. They have it pretty good. Men are made out to be pigs and that's not true or fair."

Of course, these types of remarks are emotionally violent. But many men would not accept this new terminology of E.V. and would call it hostile and inaccurate—as they often do about feminist statements in general.

Yet some men are more aware:

"I don't like the idea of treating women as less important than me, because I am a man, and using them for sex and general abuse because everyone else does. I can't, and won't, do it. It seems like an essential ethic to not fuck over women in my generation, but there are still a lot of men who do it."

Toward a New Emotional Contract

Most women feel that something is not quite right in the emotional balance of their relationships, that somehow there is a built-in power imbalance, that men say more "mean" things to them during fights, for example, than vice versa. But women have been called "paranoid" if they said they thought something unfair was going on. Many of us did not consciously label the "something wrong" as the unequal emotional contract it is, because, as we have seen, society encourages everyone to blame women. As a famous woman comedian once said, "My boyfriend and I had two things in common: we both loved him and hated me."

This general atmosphere—that it's the woman's fault if things go wrong, she is a "nag," "manipulative," or must be "impossible to live with" (the stereotyped famous "wife" jokes)—makes many of us constantly question our own perception of what is really going on. Sometimes we even think (or are told) we must be "crazy" to get so upset at "normal" things, "small details." But the reality is that our society's code of behavior reinforces some men's condescending attitudes and creates major problems in love relationships.

Can love survive without equality?

In fact, this outdated emotional contract is the major problem in most love relationships: it makes women and men into "star-crossed lovers" fated from birth to be at odds, even though they may love each other. This is not necessary. It is not written in the stars that love has to be so difficult. But we must change cultural prejudices so that our private lives can be more beautiful, peaceful and happy. No. The truism of the "ageless" "battle of the sexes" is not wisdom; rather, it is a way of explaining away a brutal division of the sexes—and we don't have to buy it. The sooner this is acknowledged, the sooner personal relationships will improve. Surely, working together, we can put an end to these unnatural prejudices and learn to enjoy our lives and our love for one another with much more happiness.

2

Is There a New Sexuality?

Sex. Where do we stand in this brave new world of sexuality? Are things better for women? Are women in the nineties going to enjoy sex more than ever before or are they tired of it after the problematic eighties? What about monogamy? Have things changed in some fundamental way for women?

AIDS and some birth control methods have increased potential health risks, and the double standard—though not as strong as it once was—is still around. Amazingly, women are still called "sluts" and "whores" and divided into categories of "good girls" and "bad girls."

The area of acceptance of women's orgasms has seen the most positive change. Since the publication of the first *Hite Report* in 1976, there is no longer the same pressure on women to have orgasm only from penetration, to fake orgasm during coitus, or to be ashamed of using clitoral stimulation for orgasm—although awkwardness may remain at times. On the other hand, the deeper question of what sexuality is is only beginning to be explored.

New Twists in the Good Old Double Standard

"Having sex shifts the power thing: when you meet the next night, why is it . . . ? You are no longer just two equals having dinner."

How can it be that this is still going on? Does the double standard still really exist? What about the New Man? Haven't most men gone beyond the old stereotype that men must "score" to be Real Men, secretly thinking that any woman who will have sex with them is a bit of a slut?

"If I had a wife who had sex outside of marriage, I am sure I would be terribly depressed and outraged. This is the worst thing that can happen to the male ego. . . . In my experience with eighty-three women with whom I have had sex outside of marriage, I had several experiences where jealousy nearly killed me. These were occasions when I learned that lovers had had sex with other men when they were ostensibly my women. Each time it was an almost unbearable affront to my belief that I am the greatest thing that ever happened in bed."

Unfortunately, many women say that although this attitude has lessened, there can be a basic change in their relationship with a man after they have had sex. Women say they feel "desired" before sex; after, they feel taken for granted and treated with less courtesy (the "had," as one woman put it). Fortunately, not all men are like this, but this is a common problem which plagues single women.

Latest lines some men love to use

Some of the current lines going around range from amazing and hilarious to insulting or just plain stupid:

"You aren't going to sleep with me? Why did you bother dressing up in all that 'please fuck me' clothing then?"

"Let's talk about you. What do you think of this bod?"

"It's the will of God."

"But I paid for dinner!"

"If we sleep together we can get rid of this sexual tension in our friendship."

"Do you have a diaphragm in?"

"I'm twenty. Isn't it sad that I'm twenty and have never gotten laid?"

"My balls hurt."

"If you get hit by a truck tomorrow, you may die without ever having slept with the best."

"Are you gay or something?"

"You say no, but I know you mean yes."

"Do you want to get a pizza and then fuck? [She slaps him.] What's the matter, you don't like pizza?"

"Want to dance? No? Well, I guess a blow job's out of the question."

"If you don't, I'll tell everyone that you did."

"I know we only just met, but I think I love you."

"You can make dinner, 'cause I'll do all the work in bed."

And finally, the classic:

"I'll still respect you in the morning!"

Snappy retorts

Some first rate comebacks women have suggested:

"Don't you remember me? I'm the one who called you pencil-dick."

"In your *dreams.*"

"No, but I'll *pay* you to go away."

"I like girls, honey."

"I have a feeling you'd disappoint me."

"Do you have a great deal of money? I'm pregnant and looking to slap a paternity suit on someone."

HIM: "Can I buy you a drink?"

HER: "No, but I'll take the cash."

"I was thinking of someone a little higher up on the food chain."

The seduction scenario and resultant games (ages 15 to 105)

The pressure to settle down and be monogamous because of AIDS is supposed to have taken the pressure off women to have sex at the drop of a hat. But this is not what most women are experiencing. They say that many men still expect sex on the first date—with no condom in sight.

"When I first went out with him, we kissed and fooled around and even though I was definitely excited, I wanted to wait for a while until we had sex, just to feel good about it. But he didn't. He was shocked when I insisted, like, 'How can a grown woman play games like a teenybopper?' "

"We had sex the first time we went out. It was in the heat of the moment. The next morning I felt anxious—I wondered if he was going to call me again. He didn't. You can't give it all away too soon if you want him to come back for more—this is the truth I finally learned."

There is also a problem of men sometimes ridiculing women for any idea that the sex they just had might be more than recreational:

"After the first time we made love, he said, 'Let's not get serious.' "

"This was a real redneck boy. Lying there in the A.M. he started to sing that song 'Freebird' to me. You know where it says, 'I'm as free as a bird, now, and this bird you cannot ch-a-a-a-a-a-a-nge.' "

"We lay there after this incredible sex and he turned to me, looking so beautiful, and said, 'Listen, babe, you seem to be taking this to heart, really serious, and I'm not. I mean, I thought we could just have some fun and there would be no demands.' "

"The sex was so romantic, he was super passionate and loving, even though I didn't know him very well. Then afterwards, he just got up and slipped on his jeans and turned on the TV. Then he tossed me my clothes and said, 'You'd better get up, my friend's coming over.' I knew then that I had been feeling this great passion all by myself."

This pressure is all too often part of a seduction scenario as old as the hills: the man tries to get sex even if he has no interest in the woman beyond one night of physical pleasure; however, he acts as romantic and flattering as possible to get the woman to go along with the plan.

Of course, not all men are like this—luckily! But certain men are more aggressive toward women, more apt to come on romantically or sexually—and this may imply something interesting about their character: they may be more insecure about their masculinity than other men.

The point here that makes this behavior reprehensible, as women point out, is that *before* sex, these men didn't state any limitations or preconditions. On the contrary, most did as much as possible to look sincere and sweet and worth having sex with. How many "New Men" practice this old-fashioned seduction behavior without even realizing it? They still accept the double standard—and their own superiority. So, as one woman said, "Don't go for a Cro-Magnon if you want Alan Alda after sex!"

Will it be a one-night stand or what?

The seduction mentality creates a double dilemma for single women; many women say that if they don't sleep with a man relatively quickly he may never call them again, but if they do sleep with him, he may not take them seriously and never call again either! This puts women in a strange and insulting position.

"So many times I've dated men who couldn't do enough for me before we slept together. They would kiss the ground I walked on! Then we would sleep together and suddenly they hardly bothered to call."

"I used to flirt with this bartender who was really handsome. Everybody wanted him, but he wanted me. I used to fantasize about how he was aching for me. So one night we did it in the ladies' room *at the bar*—it was great. But then he just zipped his jeans up and went back to work acting like I wasn't even there. I mean, I know he was working but he could at least have smiled at me. I felt powerless, like the thing that gave me my only power *over him,* my 'booty,' had been given to him and now he wasn't interested in me anymore."

"It would be so great to know that when I flirt with a guy, he is turned on, but not in a way that demeans me— just in a sexy way. And that if we 'do it' we can both be sure that we are going to be nice to each other after, no matter what, even if we only do it once and one of us decides it is not right for us, whatever the reason. Men are so arrogant—they think all women are out to catch them! But listen, guys, Sometimes we make a choice that doesn't include *you.*"

"It is so infuriating when men behave as if they don't care after the event—when *before* we had sex they were sweet and sensitive! Do they think I'm impressed? I just think they are jerks. But how can I know how they will act *after* sex until I *have* sex?"

"I started to see this young lawyer, Doug, where I work as a paralegal. I had spent a lot of time in night school and had the summer nights off—I was looking forward to going out with men again.

"I am pretty, I guess, in a sort of plain way. People don't gawk at me on the street but I have had a few men find me attractive and I feel pretty presentable most days. Mostly people like me because I'm 'fun' and 'wild.'

"When we first went out, it was a *great date.* You know, real romantic with the restaurant and the flowers, the beautiful weather, the long walk to my door. I'm a sucker for all that. He picked me up at my apartment with tulips. We went to a Japanese restaurant where there were little rooms with low tables and you had to take your shoes off.

"Right away I looked at his hands and arms when he rolled up his sleeves. I had noticed them over the past weeks when we were at work, and now the show was for me!

"He was hysterically funny which I loved, because a lot of the men at the firm are a little on the dry side. We talked about sailing, California, D.H. Lawrence, movies, dogs . . . we had a lot in common, and I felt that 'click' when things are really good with someone.

"Dinner was long and langorous and sensual. Sushi is so sensual, it's like digging your teeth into flesh. Watching him eat it was very sexy. I can't believe I'm writing this! There were some delicious pregnant silences where we just ate and grinned. Kind of *Tom Jones,* you know? I stretched my foot out under the table and it rested next to him. He touched it while we talked, lightly, in the middle of the sole of my foot, and it was excruciatingly sexy.

"We shared a chocolate mousse and then walked along the river. We stopped at this overlook and kissed kind of short and light, me standing in between his legs.

"Back at my apartment, I lit (lighted?) the candles and we sat on the floor and talked some more. Then everything happened at once. He came around the table and said, 'God, I want you,' and I mumbled something similar. As he picked me up and lay me down on the rug, he said, 'You know how when it's right, you just know it?'

"I loved it. I loved it. I was also very scared that he would wake up and think that he had gone too far (with his feelings) and pull back, disappear. I couldn't help wondering, despite all messages to the contrary, when he would 'come to' and realize that he didn't really take a woman who would fuck him on the first date seriously. I guess I'm conditioned: damned if you do, damned if you don't.

"We have seen each other again, but it's clear that this guy's passion level increases with the state of arousal he's in, because when we're not having sex he's cool as a cucumber. It's obvious that he doesn't want to fall in love with me. Or maybe it's that he couldn't, considering the 'kind of girl' I am (in other people's opinion). I wonder if I am too good in bed? Isn't that ridiculous?"

Should men be less "free," or should women be more "free"?

The unspoken message women say they receive from many men goes something like this: "If we have sex, it doesn't mean anything and shouldn't lead you to expect anything. So I might call you and then I might not, but let's not worry about that now, let the future happen when it happens. If you can't, there's something wrong with you." The rule is "stay casual, no strings attached."

In fact, although many women *do* enjoy casual sex at some time in their lives, the problem with one-night stands is the dishonesty, not being told in advance or treated respectfully after.

Why are men allowed any and all means of expressing themselves sexually—with feelings, without feelings, pushing for sex (without saying it's "only sex,") as often as they like—while women are not supposed to? Because the double standard—that "boys will be boys"—is still around. Society still encourages men to get ego boosts by having as many women as possible, and often admires them for doing so, never mind the woman's feelings.

A further insult and indication of men's status in society is that in this scenario the man defines everything on his terms: he decides if he wants to see the woman again, and he decides whether he will give her the status of "a woman to be taken seriously," "a woman to be used for sex," or "a woman to be dropped." This is a nasty form of sexism —a preconceived set of values which most men don't even realize they have—that are very difficult to fight against.

Does sexual equality mean women should be more "free" like men? Or does it mean men not pushing for sex at the drop of a hat but taking on some of women's values about sex?

Many college men talk about something called the Three Date Rule: if a man takes a woman out three times and she does not give in and sleep with him, he should move on to the next potential "conquest"—(three strikes and you're out). The problem, however, is that women say even if they *do* have sex by the third date, the man may *still* move on—because, now that he has had her, why stay?!

Try asking men you know whether they subscribe to the double standard. Most of them will probably say they don't. But then try this: ask them whether a woman they were thinking of marrying would still be as appealing if they discovered she had slept with, say, thirty men that year. Ten to one, most will say she would not be. Then ask them what they would think of a male friend who had had the same number of partners in the same amount of time (and was getting married!). Most would admit that they admire him or see nothing really wrong. The double standard, whether men realize it or not, is still going strong. In fact, stronger than ever.

If men are asked the theoretical question—"Choose between having sex with fewer women *or* accept women's right to have sex with many men"—more often than not men choose the latter. However, see how many of them would consider marrying one of those women!

Some other men, however, criticize these attitudes and would never behave these ways themselves:

"I don't get the way men are. Maybe I was raised in a really progressive atmosphere, because I think a woman has just as many rights over how many men she wants to sleep with as a man does about how many women he wants to sleep with. The only thing that *really matters* is that no one is dishonest, and no one really leads anyone on if they don't feel much."

"I'm sick and tired of all this stuff about being a Real Man in bed. I don't like to see how many women I can get. In fact, I really have to work up to the idea of having a sexual relationship with a woman. It's more satisfying that way for me."

AIDS: Has it changed many of the men you know?

Relationships in the nineties, whether they are serious or a fling, have one thing in common: they ought to begin with an HIV conversation of some kind. However, most women say that this is a very difficult thing to initiate and that heterosexual men rarely volunteer information about their sexual history or use a condom. It seems they can be just as inconsiderate about AIDS protection as they have been in the past about birth control, when the only risk was pregnancy; many men assume that a woman is on the pill or that she is using another method of contraception if she doesn't say anything: "It's none of my business as long as it doesn't get in the way." However, for protection from AIDS, the decision to use a condom has to be *mutual.*

AIDS INFORMATION

Using a condom during coitus is the *only* way for both partners to avoid contracting or transmitting HIV. There is some possibility, statistically less than for coitus, of contracting AIDS if you don't use a condom for oral sex, especially fellatio. Although it has been widely thought that stomach acids would destroy the fragile virus before it entered the bloodstream, there are new studies that refute this. Although fellatio to orgasm is the most likely to be unsafe, even fellatio just for stimulation can produce preejaculatory fluid, the drop of liquid that appears on the tip of the penis long before ejaculation. Ingestion of this could be unsafe. Also a man could contact the virus during cunnilingus.

One area of confusion about AIDS prevention is the use of lubricants during coitus and anal intercourse. What is missing from all conversations about heterosexual AIDS is the fact that heterosexuals *do* routinely engage in anal intercourse—and they are equally at risk when engaging in anal intercourse with an infected man as gay men are. But because anal sex is "taboo" for straight people, no one admits to it—but it is crucial to address the subject.

Lubricants are usually used to make anal sex more comfortable. But oil-based lubricants (such as Vaseline) can weaken the latex in a condom, causing pore-sized holes that, although invisible to the naked eye, can nevertheless transmit the AIDS virus. The only lubricants that should be used are water-based ones (such as K-Y jelly).

Women should know all of the above *without exception,* plus the fact that the riskiest time for a woman to have coitus with an HIV-infected man is during and just before menses.

Thank goodness kissing, even deep, langorous, delicious, long kissing is completely safe! So is mutual masturbation, and all sorts of fun sex. But if you have particular questions which we have not addressed, call the Gay Men's Health Crisis in New York City. They have an AIDS Info hotline, which is by no means exclusively for gay men. They are happy to answer any and all questions for you at (212) 807-6655.

Despite the spread of AIDS, unfortunately, few heterosexual men take time in the early stages of passionate embrace to say that they have a condom and plan to use it. One woman asked her lover why he hadn't raised the subject when they first slept together. "I assumed you were protected," he replied, "and that you would have told me if you had AIDS." But it is important to realize that neither of you may know that you are HIV positive, and that the days of not using a condom *are over*. Listen to some of the antiquated comments men make when asked about condoms:

"I don't sleep with unprepared women."

"I don't like condoms. Anything that does not interfere is OK."

"It feels like taking a shower in a raincoat."

"I haven't used a condom in so long I can't remember what it's like, although I often have one or two with me."

"I don't put anything on my dick."

"I'd rather just look for someone who doesn't have AIDS and is on the pill."

More and more women find that in order to protect themselves, it's necessary to take the initiative. But many women feel that this puts them in an impossible position: if they come prepared, men may think they are an "easy lay," but if they don't, then they can't depend on men to be responsible. So, as one woman puts it:

"I'd almost rather not have sex than have to deal with it —I mean, bring it up, feel weird, not trust each other."

What if AIDS is a reality for you?

Increasing numbers of women are being infected with HIV. If you are HIV positive, how will you tell potential sexual partners? Will you find it too difficult, and thus avoid sex? Not only is there personal anguish to deal with, but difficult social/sexual situations become even more strained, as this young woman describes:

"I am HIV positive. I haven't had sex in a year and a half. You cannot imagine how difficult sex has become for me. And in a way I'm not even interested in having it. It's not only that I worry about how they'd react if I told them, but I also worry because I could pass it on. Telling them is only half of it.

"I went to some counseling centers, but they were all gay males there. At first when I found out I tested positive, I panicked. I haven't told my parents. I feel alone a lot because I can't talk to anyone. I have a counselor, she tells me to drink orange juice! She doesn't know how I really feel—in the morning I shake and have huge bouts of depression. To go out, I have to put on a completely different face to how I feel.

"When I told some friends of mine they became really

abusive . . . they assumed that I had had lots of sex, that that's why I got it!

"Someone said that 'loneliness is everyone's greatest fear.' I feel really lonely sometimes. My father wants me to get married, he doesn't know. Think of it—falling passionately in love and just knowing it can never be! So meanwhile, if I'm kissing someone, I just break away.

"I never thought I would get AIDS, but I did. I want to kill the bloody bastard who did it. He didn't tell me. A one-night stand. He was a rugby player—it was just something that happened one night. I confronted him with it later. He was really surprised I knew.

"I go out and forget who I really am. I'm really mad. It's like schizophrenia, living this way. I found out I had it when I got pneumonia. At the hospital they said, 'She's only twenty and she's got pneumonia?' That's when they decided to check me out for AIDS.

"Now I'm really turned off to the idea of penetration. But I'm not attracted to women either. I find the idea of sex repulsive. I'm twenty-one, I'm young, and I'm scared of dying. I don't have time to worry about sex. I find I like being alone in an odd way. I go home and write things down. I want to be alone, and I long to be with others. I don't know, it's just an impossible thing."

Is the "new woman" allowed to resent the one-night stand?

You think one-night stands don't happen anymore? Woman after woman confirmed they are still going strong, with a full-fledged seduction scenario and no advance warning.

The problem here is that though women may also feel like having anonymous sex for one night, they do not tend to trick men into it—they will most likely say at the outset,

"This is just for fun," and not act disrespectful afterward. But women say men deceive them by *pretending* that it is more. This doesn't let women know what they are getting into.

One woman describes how she feels after being tricked:

"I come off feeling worse than if I had had no sex at all. To say 'I feel so cheap' sounds silly, but that's how I feel."

Another woman in her twenties tells how she was led to believe a man really liked her, how she was dumped by him after sleeping with him, and how she made him see how it feels to be disrespected:

"I went out with Sam twice about two months ago. The reason I went out with him in the first place was he kept telling me how beautiful I was, and I was a real sucker for it. 'Oh, you have such beautiful legs, such beautiful eyes . . .' I should have known.

"The first time, I didn't sleep with him. But the second night I stupidly did, and he never called me again.

"Then one day I ran into him on the street, and, like an idiot, invited him to a party I was giving. I didn't tell anyone except my best friend I'd invited him—because I knew everybody would pounce on me for being such a masochist. I hoped he wouldn't show up, so nobody would ever know I'd broken down and invited him. But he showed up, and I ignored him. Then we were in the kitchen and he tried to kiss me. I looked at him and said, 'Sam, why on earth would I want to kiss you? The last time I slept with you, you didn't even call me again. So why would I want to do that?' And he said, 'You're making me feel guilty!'

"So anyway, after the party, we went with some people to a coffee shop and he kept touching me and stuff, acting like I was his date. When we all left, he started kissing me on the street. I was real uninterested, but he said to me anyway, 'Do you want to make love now?' This guy is so persistent—if you say no, he just asks you again! Ten times until he sort of wears you down—that is what happened last time. And I said, 'Of course not. For what? You know how I feel, I've already told you. This is ridiculous.' He just ignored that and said, 'Don't you want to come to my place?' I said, *'No!* He then said, 'Can I walk you upstairs?' (to my apartment).

"I thought to myself, 'If he wants to be such an idiot, let him; in fact, I'll bring him upstairs, then I'll throw him out of my house.' I thought it would be fun to get my revenge. I was definitely into being a fifties cock tease and then leaving him with aching balls.

"So I brought him upstairs by the elevator. He kissed me good night, then started getting more and more passionate. We were standing by the door, in the hallway, and he undid my dress at the back and then started touching me. I thought, 'Good! Maybe he'll actually do some decent foreplay for a while and then I can have an orgasm and throw him out! What the hell, I haven't had sex in a long time, I might as well take advantage of it.'

"But as soon as I had just started to enjoy that, I looked down and suddenly he was unzipping his pants and pulling his dick out.

"Then he just barely puts it in, he's just getting the tip in there, and I say, *'stop right now!'* He immediately jumps back two feet and says, 'Why??!' (We're standing there, my dress is all undone, his pants are down on the floor around his ankles, etc.) I say, 'Look, Sam, I told you that it really bothered me when you didn't call me last time . . . why did you go to all that trouble—dressing up, taking me out to dinner and driving me places. Why didn't you just stay at home and jerk off?'

"So that was how it ended, with him being, like, stunned."

Who is the "new woman" sexually?

But wait—isn't the New Woman supposed to act like "one of the guys"? What if she doesn't want to take on a male attitude to sex, seduction mentality and all? And if she doesn't like casual sex, isn't she incredibly uncool? No. Women are saying that they would like to make their choices about sex without being labeled, and in fact develop a new kind of atmosphere around relationships with men, not keep on having to weed out the sincere sexual invitations from the seductions. Women say it's not human nature or male hormones—it's a matter of some men having a better code of honor.

Are women always serious about sex?

Of course, women like sex "just for fun," too! While women often say they prefer sex with feeling at some point in their lives, most also like to try playing around:

"I love, love, *love* to explore men's bodies! They each have a different smell and a different touch."

"I liked to have sex (now I'm married) with different men in the past to see how they made love, what they did when they came. And whether they did it once, twice, or all night long. They were all so different."

"When he walked in, I knew I was very attracted to him. He had dark, curly hair, and he looked up at me from under his brows with brilliant blue eyes. I made a mental note to thank my friend for giving him my number. This could be one hell of an evening. We had a great dinner, got a little drunk, and he suggested we go back to my place. I didn't disagree! He said he was still hungry (!). We got to my apartment and he sat in the living room looking at my bookshelves while I rummaged around in the kitchen trying to make something to eat. All I had was stale rolls, but I thought, 'What the hell, he doesn't care, he'll eat them and think they're delicious.' So I'm standing there, swaying a bit from the wine, and trying to slice these rolls in half so they can fit in the toaster.

"He came up behind me and kissed my neck. He smelled so good, his body felt so strong and lithe against my back. I forgot the rolls, I forgot I was tired from a week's work, I forgot I was in my damned kitchen.

"We went wild together and were on my kitchen floor in a matter of minutes. We both had a great time. It was total abandon—my jewelry was in the sink, my clothes were strewn all over the place, my shoes were under the stove. He left at three-thirty, which pissed me off, but it was still great and some of the steamiest sex I've ever had."

One woman remembers a fantastic night of sex with two friends:

"I was exhausted. I had been working hard and had just come home. I was not in the mood for fun.

"I had just washed my face when the doorbell rang. Keith and Brian, two friends of mine, were standing in the doorway in black tie. This is what happened:

ME: Hi . . . what are you guys doing? [With a smile and a giggle of disbelief.]
KEITH AND BRIAN: We are here to please you. [Said in a sort of robotlike fashion.]
ME: What do you mean? I look like shit, I'm exhausted, I've just gotten home . . . you want me to go out?

KEITH AND BRIAN: We are here to please you. Come with us, please.

"They walked toward me with smiles on their faces. They picked me off the floor and kept saying, 'Come with us, we are here to please you.' I started laughing uncontrollably. They carried me out to their car and put me in the front seat. They got in on either side, blindfolded me, and wrapped me in a warm blanket. They poured me a glass of very good champagne, and we took off.

"They told me jokes and gave me more champagne. Soon, we pulled over. Keith got out of the car for about two minutes. I was still blindfolded. He returned and we got out. They led me forward and then unlocked a door. Inside, they sat me down and I heard noises of clothing being taken off. They untied my blindfold. We were in a motel room. Keith and Brian stood before me in nothing but tight navy blue underwear (they are called 'rail-grabbers'!) and very wide smiles.

"Keith unzipped a small suitcase as Brian led me to the waterbed and laid me down on my stomach. They turned out the lights. Brian sat at the head of the bed and Keith sat at the foot. They started to massage me through my clothes, strongly and deeply, and they could tell I was perfectly relaxed and enjoying this.

"Soon, my shirt came off. Then my bra. They were very intent on what they were doing, totally in tune with what felt good to me and what didn't. It seemed they really *were* there to please me!

"After a while, Keith brought out a jar of honey, and they started to apply it to my skin, very slowly and sensuously. Then they started to lick it off. With both of them working on me at the same time, I was slipping into oblivion. Nothing existed at the moment but this room and the three of us—nothing else mattered. I was doing something illicit, something I had never come close to doing before and I *loved it!*

"Soon, we are all entwined with each other—I didn't know who was kissing me nor who I was kissing.

"Finally, Keith was inside me and Brian was touching me everywhere. Their hands and tongues and cocks were all over me. Then Brian was over me with his cock in my mouth while Keith pushed into me even harder. Brian moaned and came in my mouth and it tasted delicious! Then he moved Keith out of the way and licked me until I was about to explode, while Keith sucked at my nipples. I am going absolutely *crazy*—It was really exciting, like my ultimate fantasy. I felt completely saturated with sex and delirious with pleasure. When it was over, we fell into an exhausted sleep.

"The next morning they took me home. I looked like I had not only been dragged through a hedge but lived in the hedge for the evening and had been hit by a very large truck. My face was chapped from their beards. I still wonder if it really happened!"

Do women today want to be monogamous?

Actually, yes and no; but it is not always a conscious choice in the real world. For example, think about when a woman goes out with one man, has sex with him, decides she doesn't like him, and/or he never calls again; then she goes out with a second man, has sex with him; then the first one calls back, she feels like seeing him, they get together, and so on? This leads, ultimately, to multiple sexual partners. As one woman asked, "How many men can you sleep with at the same time without being a slut?"

What is a slut, anyway? When looking at our postsexual revolution ideas, it is important to take a larger worldview and realize that, historically, women with many lovers have been considered "generous" (Chaucer's Wife of

Bath), "heroic" (Cleopatra), and so on. Why does our culture think they were heroic and generous while we judge
women today with multiple partners "loose," "immoral,"
"slutty"? In other words, less than men who can do it and
be called Casanovas, Don Juans—successful.

If a woman wants monogamy, how is she supposed to "bring it up" with a new man?

"I think it's more important than ever to want monogamy. I always did, but now, with AIDS in the world, I
can't imagine a relationship without it. But I can just imagine the quizzical looks I would get from men if, before the
first time I sleep with them, I would say, 'I think we should
both get HIV tests and then not sleep with anyone else.'
They would act like, 'What gives her the right to make
demands like that?' I always wanted to demand monogamy. It's weird to now have a pandemic on my side."

Most women want their boyfriends and lovers to be *as
monogamous as they themselves are*—as opposed to some
men's double standard in which it is acceptable, in fact well
thought of, for men to have more than one partner, but
not for the women they sleep with to do the same.

One woman wrote to her lover about how bad she feels
about his "secretive" affairs:

"I can't live with the knowledge that you are thinking of
and possibly actually fucking others behind my back. That
you would/could try and brainwash me into believing that
it was just a one-time thing, then Hope comes up, then
Robin comes up—God knows who else was with you—is
incredible to me. That you could lie to me is incredible.
But what is really incredible is that you should *want* that. I
have found myself craving sexual and emotional attention
from men lately, but I know I only feel that way because I

don't have it from you. I want it so much from you, but you are not there for me (really, or consistently), so I look for it in others, at least the possibility of it anyway. But for you? Why you need others is something I find hard to comprehend. The line about your French blood (that French men need mistresses) is the stupidest thing I have ever heard, so I'm not even going to go into that."

But women don't always want monogamy:

"My friends can't understand how I can be happy to love a man who sleeps with other women. I sleep with other men, too. They think it's strange and that we 'just *think* we're happy.' But we really are! I feel guilty sometimes for not agonizing over this the way they would like me to. It seems as though, even though I've reached success in my career, I somehow have failed in my personal life if I'm not in a monogamous relationship."

"Even with the advent of AIDS, I still am not ready to have a monogamous relationship. I just don't want one. I want to be free to have sex with whomever I choose, and I don't feel it's right to ask a man for that freedom without giving him the same freedom. It's funny, but it's harder than you think to find men who will go for this. They want to be able to screw around, but they don't want you to! I do insist that they tell me if they sleep with someone, and that they are confident about that person's sexual history, and I tell them the same."

Date rape

The pressure to have sex is at its worst when it reaches the stage where, even though you may be on a date with a man, you have to give in to sex to keep him nonviolent. This is a form of rape, a violation of your desires and body —date rape:

"I definitely didn't want to sleep with him the first night, it was just too soon. It never occurred to me that he would put up a fight about it. I thought he liked me. He started to hold me down with one arm and unzip his fly at the same time. I laughed at first because I thought he was just playing. But then I realized that what I wanted was of no importance to him—in fact he wasn't even thinking about it. I said no, again and again, but it was clear he wasn't going to stop, and he was big. I was scared to kick him or put up a fight, and I was confused. This had been a nice guy that I really liked, and he was forcing me to have sex against my will. I let him. I had been slightly aroused from kissing him (before he started to push), but now all I felt was dirty and sad."

"I really liked this man, so I agreed to have dinner with him. We had a nice time, but when the bill came, he offered me 'dessert at his place.' I went because I couldn't imagine he would try the old 'let's see how fast I can get her in the sack' routine—he seemed such a gentleman. When we got there he dimmed the lights and put some jazz on the stereo and got me some ice cream. Then he sat next to me. Then he lay next to me and all the time I'm thinking, 'Oh, I'm so disappointed this is happening,' but I knew that if I said something he would tell me I had hang-ups and it would turn into a big scene. We work for the same company, so I was worried about that. So I lay there and tried to continue talking but it was clear he only had one thing on his mind. I gave up and let him get on with it."

Another woman recalls a vivid experience of date rape:

"I was with a group of people, many of whom I did not know. I was depressed over the failure of a relationship and had just stopped by for a quick hello. Then I noticed a very attractive blond man who kept looking at me and smiling. I thought he had a nice smile, but I wasn't that interested. It was too much effort to be animated!

"I walked over to get a cup of coffee, and he was there immediately. He was very talkative, introduced himself and chatted with me. He seemed bright and interesting. It was really nice to feel someone found me attractive and interesting when I had recently had such a blow to my heart and ego.

"We went out to the corner for a cup of coffee and talked for a while. He told me he had just divorced and had a little daughter whom he loved. He was a fashion photographer. We found that we knew some people in common. I was getting more and more interested, energized by his attention. He asked me back to his house.

"To this day, I can't believe I went. I don't know what I was thinking, I had only just met him. I would never normally do that. I guess I was in a what-the-hell mood and was feeling so sad and crazy that my judgment was off. Very off.

"We got to his place and went inside. It was comfortable and pleasant. He showed me photographs and they were really quite good. He had a very childlike quality, very appealing. He got excited over everything we talked about.

"He suggested we watch *Star Trek IV*, which I thought was just about the most boring thing I could imagine. I was here with this trendy, hip fashion photographer and he wanted to watch *Star Trek IV!*

"He pulled my chair next to his and kissed me a little. It was nice. He touched me and that was nice too. As he started to lift up my dress, I said I really had to go home. He said, 'No, you don't,' and kept going. I stood up, but he pulled me back down very violently and said, 'God, are you hung up or something? I mean, we met, we like each other, what's the matter? Don't you ever have any fun? What's the matter with you?' He was shouting and his face scared me.

"I couldn't believe it. I mean, I had heard about these kinds of things happening to other women, but I never thought it would happen to me.

"I told him that it was nothing to do with having fun. I said that I would feel lousy about it in the morning, and, anyway, didn't he know it was 1989 and there was a disease called AIDS that was killing everybody, and how could we have sex so casually? He sort of rolled his eyes and said, 'Oh, God, *that*' (pointing to his crotch) 'is clean. Don't worry, I mean, I have a healthy daughter, I've been married for five years.'

I was going to say that that had nothing to do with it because it didn't tell me who his wife had slept with while they were married and who he had slept with since his 'monogamy' had expired, but it just wasn't worth it, he wasn't going to hear any of that.

"He gave me such a hard time that I ended up jerking him off just so he would leave me alone and let me out of the apartment (he had locked the door)."

Date rape is an extremely serious issue, with a rapidly increasing number of women reporting such occurrences, not only on college campuses, but in urban, suburban, and rural areas. The current climate of "upholding family values" is doing nothing to encourage men to think about what they are doing, nor question why they still pressure women into sex. The pressure, as usual, is on women to modify *their* behavior: to learn to say no, dress less suggestively, and so on. While knowing how to say no is very important, why is it still assumed that men's behavior is "normal" and ours is due to "psychology"? And does a 'no' really stop men anyway? It is not deep-seated conflict that drives us to say no and mean yes—we say no when we want the man to stop what he is doing—and we mean no!

The end of the silence

Though most people would say that date rape is a "new phenomenon," this is incorrect. What *is* a new phenomenon is the recognition of these acts by society. This is due to the realization that date rape *is* rape. Fewer and fewer women are remaining silent; their voices are growing louder and louder. Women's confidence in the fact that nothing they did *asked for rape or caused rape* increases every day. And it is clear that "female masochism" as an explanation is completely wrong. The idea that women look for suffering until they find it is absurd.

Eighty percent of the rapes in this nation are acquaintance rapes; that is, the woman either knows the man as a friend or relative or she is going out on a date with him. Eighty percent! Thus, there is usually some level of trust established.

It is clear from the statistics that a woman is more likely to be raped by someone she knows than by a stranger jumping out of a darkened doorway. This is shocking but nevertheless true. So, unfortunately, women must be more prepared to doubt men, not to fully trust—which is tragic. Still, to have all the tools for evading rape that are possible, a woman should always think through how she might deal with a potential rape or assault in that situation.

Of course, we can't mistrust everyone who has a penis! But we can try to be more aware of those times when we have an unsafe feeling around someone "for no reason." We should set our own limits whether we know a man well or not.

Remember, women are not responsible for any form of rape whatsoever. True, sometimes women make huge errors in judgment (like anyone else), but stupidity does not license, does not entitle, and does not grant permission to rape.

Is it true that "rape is not sex" to men? That instead of being about lust and sexual drive, rape is about hatred and violence? This is a complex question; however, when you look at the way violence and sex are meshed in our society, the answer is clearer. Men are virtually encouraged to rape from boyhood. As boys, men are taught to "go out and take what you want," "don't take no for an answer." Most men are not told anything other than the fact that women are to be conquered.

Rape crisis centers advise women that there are two clues to both batterers and rapists. First, the majority are extremely possessive and treat women as property. Second, they are hypercritical of women. There is a distinct Dr. Jekyll and Mr. Hyde quality to the acquaintance or date rapist; often he is charming and disarming until he rapes, when women frequently describe him as turning into a monster. Psychologists who deal with ritualistic abuse survivors report that these women sometimes split into multiple personalities to survive the horror of what was done to them, the theory being that "troops" can handle the horror better than just one little girl on her own.

Date rape on college campuses is an important issue discussed by the media these days. But many women at college in the sixties and seventies will tell you that it was happening then too, although was not considered rape:

"I was a freshman at State College in 1972 and wanted a group of friends to pal around with. I hung out with other girls on my floor and we went to a particular frat house for Wednesday night keg parties. It was a beautiful old building on a hill, built in about 1890 I suppose. It had books all around, leather chairs, wood paneling and even a real fireplace. Downstairs was the bar and it was always crowded with people by about nine o'clock, which was when I would usually get there.

"We all went there one night in the spring. The freshmen were about to begin rush week, where the guys try to get into the fraternity they want to belong to. It was crazy there, loud music, wild dancing, cute guys, cute girls. It was great!

"I was dancing with some friends of mine when a sophomore I knew from class pulled me aside and said he had something to ask me. We went into the library and got new beers and sat down. He was a member of the frat, and was head of the freshman rush week. He explained an old tradition that this frat had had for fifty years: a girl was found who was considered very sexy and wild, and she had to perform certain duties the night of the rush party, at which only members and 'pledges' were in attendance. I asked him what the girl had to do, and he said; 'Oh, they don't *have* to do anything, it's actually an honor, only fifty girls have ever been asked and they all said yes.' I said, 'So what did they do?'

"He said that she had to get dressed in a corset, garters, leather jacket, high-heeled boots, and be at the party as the rush mascot, and that was about it. 'You know, she has to look really horny and hot, but it's just to impress the pledges and drive them crazy, that's all. But this is a totally secret ritual, and you can't tell anyone or we'll have to cancel you. Anyway, we voted and want you to do it. Okay?'

"I was so flattered (plus I kind of liked him) and so I said I would do it and actually looked forward to the initiation night. My social life would be certain from then on.

"Pledge night came and I showed up in my getup under a long raincoat. I was hustled up to a secret room in the top of the building, with a secret door and a secret passageway and all. In the secret room were all the frat members in cloaks and carrying candles. In the corner stood twenty nervous pledges in their underwear, cracking up and being told to shut up by the members.

"What came next is a blur—I've tried to remember it but I just can't very well. Someone grabbed my arms from behind and started talking to me about how I wanted this and now I was going to get it, and how much they all wanted to see these kids fuck me. They were really hurting my arms and I couldn't breathe too well because I was really scared. My heart was beating really loud and I thought I might faint. I couldn't believe what was happening, but I knew it was.

"I don't know whether they all raped me or not. I was crying so hard after the third one that I had my eyes closed and didn't know when one got up and the other one came down on top of me. All I know was that I was in there for what seemed like hours and then I was left alone with a blindfold on (this they put on sometime during the rapes) and I lifted it and looked down at my ripped lingerie and my swollen and bruised legs and pelvis. I got out and went back to my dorm and skipped classes for two days.

"I dropped out of State and went to college in Colorado and did pretty well. I am married now to the greatest guy. But sometimes I wake up in the middle of the night and think about this. My husband doesn't know. I guess I've just tried to live as though it never happened."

We cannot stress strongly enough how important it is to take seriously your situation when you are with men who make you feel uncomfortable—even men who are familiar, friends, "gentlemen." And even when the events are harmless and fun. Be aware! *You* are more important and more valuable than being afraid to offend someone by seeming not to trust him or wanting to protect yourself.

Sexuality: Redefining It

Are men and women sexually at odds?

Women often value different sexual activities than men. For example, most women enjoy clitoral stimulation at least as much as intercourse and certainly orgasm more easily from it. But most men are more focused on intercourse.

One woman describes her current struggle to express her sexuality with her boyfriend:

"My anger with him began very quickly with the first intercourse. First, I was resistant to sex at that moment, and felt that he ignored this in his typically male intense desire to complete the act, as if that would couple us even without my cooperation. I feel that fucking is much more pleasurable for him than for me, that the whole system is geared toward the pretense that fucking is the epitome of sexuality.

"I've told him that I don't usually orgasm from intercourse and that when I do, it's less intense and satisfying than a clitoral orgasm. I've been telling him this for almost two years. He keeps trying to think of it as a temporary condition—because otherwise, he says, it ruins something for him. He always dreamed of finding a woman who would respond to him, to his penis. He says this is something that takes away the whole pornographic, sadistic image of the man as taking, and makes him a giver.

"What I keep trying to tell him is that it wouldn't matter to me—that I'd be more than happy to give in that way—if he would accept *my* sexuality as it is. I've never felt accepted by him for what feels best to me; we are always at cross-purposes and trying to accomplish the impossible.

"I feel guilty for not coming from fucking. I'm afraid he's going to leave me for someone who'll pretend to come from fucking, who'll lie, or who doesn't know any better. He feels guilty for wanting the turn-on of a woman who really loves fucking. The funny thing is that what turns me on most about fucking is how good it feels to him.

"I'd like to ask women how they live with men, how they enjoy sex, until I get some real answers. I've talked about not coming from intercourse with two or three women—it makes me mad that men can have such reliable pleasure from sex and we can't. Usually from women I get the feeling that it's just one of those things they've learned to live with."

To have sex on "his" terms?

One of the worst pressures women feel is the pressure to disregard their own needs, whether physical, emotional, or psychological, to please men in bed.

"I often feel pressured into sex by my lover. Also pressured in liking sex—being told that what feels good to him ought to be my primary satisfaction. I pressure myself. I often try to make my vagina please me, but without real confidence that it can. I do it to end the tension of his wanting sex, to maintain the relationship despite my doubts, to justify my anger against him. The pressure to be open to whatever feels good to the man is sometimes overwhelming."

"I like this man so much and want him to like me as much that I'll do almost anything. It makes me very embarrassed to say this. But I will. If he wants me to dress up in weird clothes or talk to him about other women and things when we are having sex, I do it. I wish I was enough."

"I learned very early on that pleasing a man in bed was a primary source of power, if not my only one. I learned as much as I could, acting the way I found men liked, learning from them what they wanted me to do, be, say. It was a worthwhile pursuit; this was a very powerful skill to have. But I was having sex and pleasing men for four years before I even knew what it felt like to have an orgasm with a man."

"I hate getting up from bed, sweaty and exhausted, having nearly killed myself with acting as though I was in ecstasy, having to go into the bathroom and 1) clean up, and 2) make myself come before going to sleep. I wonder if other women feel like this."

"I have to act as though it's OK with me if he just decides to get up and leave because there's a good game on TV and he wants to watch it with his friends! That is *not* OK with me. It's not very romantic."

"My lover is very sensitive, but I think it would really upset him to know I don't get as turned on as he thinks I do when we make love. I want to tell him, but it's too late now. Now our sex life is set. I was so worried that he would leave and find someone else that I faked it every time. Now I can't stop, or maybe he might leave. I couldn't bear that."

What is male sexuality—really?

Do we really know what male sexuality is? While the pressure is stereotypically on women (as usual) to adapt to men's sexual needs, is the definition of men's needs really as cut and dried as everyone seems to believe? The definition of male sexuality as a driving desire for penetration is clearly exaggerated; male sexuality could comprise a much larger, more varied group of physical feelings than erection, penetration, and ejaculation. Some men, in fact, have expressed just this idea:

"Sex is just jerking off into a hole if there is no touching, kissing, and smiling and noises. I might as well be alone. I don't even have to come all the time if I'm with the right woman."

"I love to feel as much of her on me as possible—feet, hands, mouth, groin, belly, chest—ah, beautiful."

However, men are socially channeled into expressing their sexuality in only reproductive ways. Not only is there enormous pressure on women to provide sexual services for men, but men are also continually expected to pressure women for sex as traditionally defined: penetration. This is not fair to men or women. The definition of sex as foreplay followed by vaginal penetration (why not call it penile covering?) and ending with male orgasm is too rigid and too cut and dried; it should be replaced by an individual vocabulary of activities to be chosen by a person at a given time to express his or her feelings.

There are many ways to express and enjoy sexuality,

some genital and some not. Historically, coitus was not always the exclusive definition of sex. In classical Greece men had sex with other men—so much so that they had to be reminded to have sex with their wives "at least three times a month"—for fear that they would not reproduce. But even here we see an emphasis on genitalia that need not always be present in a more sensual definition of sexuality.

Toward a more erotic sexuality

So, what is sex? Is it reproductive activity only? Is intercourse the only natural definition of sex? For example, is it sex when no "vaginal penetration" takes place? Intercourse became the basic definition of sex (as put forth in *The Hite Report on Male Sexuality*) because at the beginning of patriarchal religion it was considered crucial that lineage go through men: reproductive activity (intercourse) was the focus of attention, touted as the most "special" of all acts of intimacy.

However, sex could be seen as an individual vocabulary of gestures and feelings—different for each person and in each relationship—if it were not for this constant emphasis on "doing it":

"I have fantasies and desires but it seems like there's only one way I'm supposed to have sex (either underneath or riding on top) and anything else would be too Intensely Weird—such as kissing naked in bed for a long time without putting it in."

So, notice during sex: is this really what you want to be doing? Or is there some other kind of physical expression you might prefer? How do *you* really feel?

Questions to ask yourself

A good way to think honestly about what sex means to you is to ask yourself the following questions:

- What is sex with your partner usually like? Do you enjoy it? Do you usually come? When?
- Which is the easiest way for you to come: masturbation, clitoral stimulation, oral sex, intercourse? Do you like your legs open or closed? Does your lover know this?
- If you don't come from intercourse, have you told a woman friend about this? How did it feel to tell her?
- Have you told your lover if you don't come from intercourse? How did he react? Did you tell him that most women don't? How did that make you feel?
- Have you ever masturbated with a lover? How did it feel to do that? Was it a turn on? If you haven't done this, would you like to?
- When do you feel the most passionate? How do you show this? Do you become more aggressive? Or do you want to be "taken"? Do you like playing different roles?
- Do you use fantasies to help you come? Which ones?
- Do you masturbate when your lover is not around? Do you think about him, or other fantasies? Do you tell him this?

- What do you think of pornography? Do you like it? If so, do you prefer literature, photos, or films? Do you like to watch/read with your lover? Does he look at it alone? How does that make you feel?
- Do you feel turned on in emotionally intense moments or do you prefer sex in quiet, cozy, safe moments?
- Would you rather have sex or a great dinner out?
- How do you feel about going down on your lover? Do you feel like it is an act of love? Do you feel in control? Does it turn you on? Or do you feel used?
- Do you prefer manual stimulation of your clitoris or oral? Do you feel uncomfortable asking your lover for oral sex? Why?
- Do you like to hear "I love you" during sex? Do you like to say it?

Questions to ask your lover

- Where do you *really* feel your orgasm? At the tip of your penis? At the base? Inside your body? Where?
- Would you still like sex if you couldn't have head-to-toe body contact during it? Would you like sex without kissing?

- How often do you have sex just because you want to come? Do you think it is more manly to have intercourse than to masturbate?
- Do you enjoy sex without vaginal penetration?
- How do you feel if I go into the bathroom and wash after you come inside me? Do you think I'm being fastidious, or do you think I think you're dirty? Do you prefer it if I don't wash afterward?
- Would you rather I went down on you or had intercourse? Why?
- Do you worry that you might have AIDS? Do you worry that I might have AIDS? Do you think that we should both have a test?
- Do you ever masturbate when I'm not around? If you do, how often do you do it? What do you think about?
- Do you think my period is exciting, boring or disgusting? What are your biggest fears about it? Do you mind getting my blood on you or the bed? Do you want to avoid oral sex during it?
- Do you feel that it is normal for a woman to come from intercourse alone? Do you feel bad if I don't? Resentful? Guilty? Do you wonder what to do next?
- Do you feel confident giving me an orgasm with your hand on my clitoris? Do you ever feel impatient when I'm getting physical stimulation and you're not? What do you think about?

- How do you feel if I make myself come? Are you turned on? Bored? Upset?
- How do you feel about the fact that many women need to have their legs together to come? Would you like to know more about women's anatomy?

Eroticism is a vast, largely unexplored area which includes the desire not only to have orgasm, but to "lie together, to press bodies together, tightly, as tightly as possible; to lie feeling the other breathe as they sleep, their breath grazing your cheek and mingling with your own; to smell their body, caress their mouth with your mouth, know the smell and taste of their genitals, to feel your finger inside them, to caress the opening of their buttocks, to lose yourself in all the feelings there are."*

* From *The Hite Report On Male Sexuality,* Alfred A. Knopf, 1981.

3

Fighting: A Radical New Look

"We have so many horrible scenes. They happen at his place or at mine, or on the phone in the middle of the night. I often wish I had a tape recorder to record the things he says and what goes on, because later he denies most of what he said, but I always remember him behaving really mean."

"He stalked out of the house breaking pottery he had made. He was totally 'out of control' and I let him rage awhile and then held him and told him how glad I was he finally 'let go.' His biggest fear was that I really didn't like him. He always said that first when we fought through these conflicts. I was really overwhelmed, sad, and angry, but on some level I knew he had to get a lot of stuff out."

Behind Closed Doors

Fighting belongs to a private world—something painful that usually happens between two people when they are alone. No one else is there, so no one knows exactly what goes on. In these moments it is difficult to perceive the dynamics of the situation clearly, see how to stop what is going on, or get a fair airing of one's feelings.

In this chapter we will strip away the isolation, end the "unseen" nature of what goes on. We will lay bare the patterns as women describe them. Renaming them realistically is the first step in changing them, so that women will have a different way of fighting, of reacting to critical situations in their relationships in the nineties.

"Are fights this bad for others?"

Women talk to each other about fights they have had, but even if their friends are sympathetic and say they know what it's like, many women still won't tell even their best friends the worst parts of what's going on for fear of being thought less of. They wonder if anyone else's fights are really as bad as theirs.

Fights feel like a private jungle where there are no rules, no outside observers, and no clear "truce" or "victory"— and they often leave women feeling very isolated and alone:

"When I fight with my husband I feel so alone. I usually wind up feeling fairly destroyed too. It starts when he hurts my feelings, which is something I do too sometimes, but when I tell him and hope he will apologize (take it back, say he didn't mean it), he gets mad and says I'm causing trouble, I'm nagging him, and he won't have it. Then I get more upset and scream at him or cry. He just gets silent and refuses to talk at all. I feel like a banshee and that I should be ashamed for screaming, and I feel ashamed of what he did to me, too. Plus, I think I look neurotic. Finally, I want so much for it to be over, I end up apologizing. I feel terrible."

"It was six months since we had had our first date, and I wanted to do something special, so I went out after work and got white balloons and streamers and put them all over my bedroom and bed. I bought a sexy lingerie outfit in white lace with garters and everything like that. He walked in and was totally nonplussed and said something like it looked 'nice,' not that I looked nice, and said he was really tired from work and was just going to go to sleep. He didn't stop to realize I would be upset by that. I lay there in the dark and cried so hard I thought my eyes were going to pop out of my face. At six in the morning, I got up and tore all the balloons and streamers down. I couldn't wait to throw them away. I felt so angry with myself for putting them up at all. When he heard me and woke up, he asked me why I was so upset. I looked at him and said that all I had wanted that night was for him to show he appreciated me. It wasn't his fault he was tired, but couldn't he have been nice about what I'd done? I had worked all day, I was tired too! Well, then he went off into his tirade about me, that I'm too demanding, have high expectations (unreasonable ones), should 'let it go,' like my feelings were invalid and unnecessary. As usual, I yelled back a little and choked back some tears and then just went to work."

"We go round and round in our fights. The other day I said I didn't want to get together. I wanted to stay home and read the paper and watch TV by myself. He was furious. Then the whole thing started as usual: 'Why can't you see me tonight and do that another night? You really are so selfish.' In the end I gave in and let him come over and watch some stupid thing on TV that I hated. Our fights are never resolved, he always gets his way, and I end up crying in the bathroom in the middle of the night while he gets his beauty sleep after a good screw."

Women often feel they should be "together" enough to stop fighting like this, so they hide their quarrels like a secret shame. In fact, the most common way of dealing with the problem is to try to hide it from outsiders so that nobody will know. The implicit meaning behind this is that if people know what is going on, they will think she must somehow be "weak" and "deserve it," or else why did she pick him?

The Pattern of Events During a Fight

This, then, is the pattern: home-grown male distancing —which puts the woman in the position of having to work to keep the emotional channels open—escalates into emotional battering or violence if the man feels seriously threatened by the woman's attempts to change the relationship, to make it more equal.

Why most fights start

Sometimes small disagreements or hurt feelings can turn into something major because of an underlying fear on the part of one or both people that the other doesn't really love them, "hates" them, is going to reject them. But with goodwill this can be resolved as mutual assurances are given. Usually that is all a person really needs, and he or she is far more able to accept a conflict and reach a resolution after that.

However, there are other types of fights. While we can all be nasty at times, it is extremely common for fights to begin with the small acts of emotional aggression and emotional bullying that women described in chapter 1. After a woman has noticed a series of such incidents, or feels vaguely uncomfortable but is not really sure why, she may try to bring up the problem or describe how she is feeling.

This often leads to the next stage of a potential fight: the man denying there is a problem or refusing to discuss the issue, whether through stony silence or a series of condescending putdowns.

For example, if a woman "complains" (tries to bring up a problem for discussion), she may be asked, "Why are you making waves? I feel fine," or told, "Now don't start like a nagging, complaining woman. I thought you were different," or, "I don't know what's wrong with you, I didn't *do* anything."

"When I am upset because of one of his condescending remarks, and say so, it's always, 'It's just a *word,* babe.' Or if today's problem is that I cooked a lovely meal for him and he didn't say anything about it, it's, 'Hey, it was good, I ate it, OK?' I can't make him see that these things are not little things to me. The things I think are the most important, he thinks are the least important. I know men and women are different, and he may never think that what I think matters matters. But when we've had the discussion before, why can't he do it for my sake? To love me?"

"When I want to talk about something that's bothering me in the relationship, he looks beleaguered, starts rolling his eyes—'Oh, poor me, badgered by this bitch.' He tells me I 'jump all over him' for 'no reason'! But I'm telling him there *is* a reason, *I* am upset!"

One man exemplifies this:

"It's so *stupid* to talk about problems every damn day. Why does she have so many?"

It's hardly surprising that women in relationships like these feel angry, hurt, and unsettled when the men who supposedly love them ignore their attempts to talk things over—even refuse to listen!

This, then, leads to a further escalation of the situation. The woman is now experiencing a double hurt or injustice. Probably at this point she is upset and is beginning to show it.

What happens then? Many men, unfortunately, buy into the social convention that women are "overemotional." When they see a woman upset, they are apt to tell her she is "overreacting"—they will probably neither listen to what she is saying nor consider her point of view to be as valid as their own. Many men do not seem to realize the self-serving and convenient nature of the stereotypes they are accepting and using.

Being put down for raising the issue

Although there *are* women who say that communication is good in their relationships, most describe being hurt and upset when they meet a brick wall of indifference or an aggressive refusal to talk during these "discussions." What many call "man-bashing" is actually a blatant reversal of the facts; women are silenced all the time when trying to communicate with men.

"When I try to bring something up, he says 'Don't even *start.*' He says those words to me before I've even begun."

"I can't seem to feel safe to say anything that's bothering me. He either tells me I don't make sense, that I'm crazy, or that he 'really can't take this anymore' (as though he will leave me if I keep it up). I feel it wouldn't happen if he'd just listen. Then it could be resolved between us and we would be closer, and happy. The way it is, it either snowballs until I am crying very hard at home or, worse, in front of him, and then I get quiet and totally submissive, just to keep the peace."

One woman tells an amazing story of how the man she loved blocked communication in a particularly hurtful way:

"I was telling him I was pregnant. It was very hard for me to make the words come out, I was so nervous and felt so sick. All he did was look at me and say, 'How do I know it's mine?' I couldn't believe it. It was the last thing I expected, or needed, to hear."

The man's indifference to this woman's feelings is a form of emotional violence. It is also typical in that it shows how some men change the subject or the focus or "miss the point" in a way that wounds the other person. As we saw in chapter 1, there are many forms of E.V., but they all involve aggressive or indifferent acts of one form or another. To be sure, women are also capable of E.V.— but studies show over and over again the large discrepancy between abusive men and abusive women; the men win hands down.

However, we can laugh about some of these situations— they can be pretty funny when you think about them later. Let's look at the most common reactions women say they encounter in fights; it's impossible not to be amused.

Seven Crazed Reactions Men Have When Women Bring Up Problems

"I feel fine. Why are you complaining?"

Many women find men can be maddeningly unresponsive to any hint of a grievance or complaint. As one said:

> "His attitude when I am upset is usually, 'I feel fine. Why are you complaining?' Or, if I keep on and get really upset, he will say, 'You're causing scenes.' Or he'll say, 'Why do you have to insist on making your point?' to which I say, 'I'm not "insisting"—I'm trying to talk to you!'"

In other words, the man in this scenario is saying he doesn't care or doesn't want to know about what the woman is saying. Even without bothering to listen to her, he believes that she is wrong:

> "It's always *me* that has 'all the problems,' it's never him. He says I always want to 'drag things up.' It never occurs to him that my being upset has something to do with what he did! He thinks it's all my own weird hang-ups."

Implicit in this attitude is the idea that the woman is always finding something *wrong* with the man, or *trying* to find things to criticize (as if this were fun!), and that if she wouldn't keep "creating" problems, everything would be fine:

"His opinion is that I am criticizing him whenever I try to bring up anything that's bothering me, or that he has done to hurt me. He tells me I am just making trouble. He doesn't listen to what I'm saying. Usually I try to talk to him calmly first, and get no response, so then I yell and he tells me I am attacking him. I can't win. I look at my behavior when he is hurt and tells me about it, and I know that I make it easy for him to talk. Why can't he do the same for me?"

The silent treatment

Men often try to shut women up with the classic silent treatment. The result is that women either shout and fights ensue, or they too become silent and cold. Either way, the problem may never be resolved:

"Until he 'resigns' himself to a talk, I meet with resistance all the way . . . I am talking and talking and getting little uh-hmms."

"What happens usually is I get mad about something and try to tell him. He says nothing. I get worked up trying to get him to talk to me, and then he says, 'What do you want from me?' which makes me even more mad because he's not saying how he feels or even reacting to what I'm talking about!"

"He could just as well be a stuffed dummy for all the communication I get from him. He just looks at me and says nothing. Absolutely nothing. And, after I've worked myself up into a tantrum trying to talk with him, if I stop for a few seconds (having asked him a question for the

50th time), he says, 'Have you finished?' AAAAAAAAA-AGH!''

"I do the talking, he just sits there and grunts. Then I yell, and he grunts some more."

"He has a classic pose. He sits immobile, looking 'above it all'—his Mussolini pose, I call it. Aloof, while I try to get through to him."

"Male nagging is silent. Silent sulking or silent, arrogant disapproval."

"I usually decide just to choke down my anger and resentment because when I bring it up he gets so furious and it always ends up being really bad."

Pretending it never happened

Women also talk about how they feel when the man in their life "deals" with something they bring up by simply ignoring the fact that they have said anything:

"I was very angry about something the other night before a couple were coming over for dinner. It was awful to see him slide right on through the evening as though nothing had happened. I am always amazed by that. Either he should join the Royal Shakespeare Company or he is the coldest and most two-faced person I have ever met. When they left, he was all cuddly and sweet and wanted to make love. I felt *totally* depressed."

"We were on the phone. I was telling him that I needed some time alone with him. I thought he would welcome this talk and be eager to help (fat chance). He glossed over the whole thing as though I had never said it and went on to mention a party we were invited to on Friday night."

Changing the subject

Many men try to change the subject in a variety of ways if they don't want to discuss something:

"When something is bothering me and I am trying to talk about it, he'll say, 'I'm sorry,' (as if that settles it) and then (briskly), 'Now let's talk about something more pleasant!' and proceeds to ignore any response I might have. This makes me see red. It is an aggressive act on his part, as I see it. But if I say so or get upset, he says, 'I don't know what you're talking about. *I'm* not shouting or fighting like *you.*' Or sometimes he kisses me, hoping that will shut me up."

"He will sit there and pick up the TV guide when we are talking and start reading it. Or look at the TV screen the entire time I am talking. When I complain, he looks at me with this expression of disdain or disbelief and says he doesn't know what I mean. Then he turns back to the TV and starts watching again."

"He'll do anything to get out of the conversation: make a phone call, go to the fridge and look in it to see what he can eat, look through his diary. I only wish he would stop everything and talk to me until our conversation was over. I don't know how he can think it will 'go away' if he ignores me. I mean, isn't it obvious that if someone needs to talk to you, the problem will remain static, unresolved until they *do* get a chance to talk to you?"

Sometimes men deny that a problem exists at all—even while a woman is screaming that there is something wrong!

"He was meeting my mother for the first time and I was nervous. He thinks it's funny to be rude sometimes, but I thought it's my mom and all, he must want her to like him. Well, he was *awful* and behaved like a ten year old. I was really upset, but later, when I tried to bring it up, he looked at me from under the covers and said, 'Go to sleep, you're tired, I was nice, you're imagining all this.' He always says it's my problem if I'm upset, never admits that there's anything wrong or that he might be wrong. God forbid!''

"We were in the car and I was trying, for the umpteenth time, to talk about the way his best friend ignores me. It really hurts me that my boyfriend doesn't stick up for me over something like this, because the coldness of his friend is so obvious. But he still said, 'You've got it wrong—Jerry really likes you.' I was so frustrated by this that I grabbed the wheel and steered the car off the road a little, almost crashing us! I did get his attention (!) but then we had a huge fight. It didn't do any good.''

In addition to all this, if a woman insists on talking about the problem, a man will often tell her she is being 'petty.' Of course, this will only make her angrier, because his attitude in itself is a sign of condescension and proof that he is not interested in what she is saying. He does not value the relationship enough to worry and wonder about what could be on her mind:

"We sometimes fight in the morning before work. Then we have to leave quickly because we're running late. So

I'm distracted all day and feel sad, dreading the moment when I have to go home. If I try to look at the argument objectively during the day, control my anger, and try to see his side, we can sometimes have a *productive* argument and get beyond it. But by five thirty he has usually decided to forget the fight and I am left with all these things unsaid, feeling as though he doesn't even care enough to work through it."

"You're an idiot for saying I hurt you"

Another common response might be called "irrational aggression," or "bullying the person you just cut down." In other words, another way men frequently try to shut women up is to attack the woman who says her feelings are being hurt—just because they are hurt and she has the nerve to tell him about it.

In this self-righteous pattern, the man attacks the woman because she "makes him feel guilty":

"We were on vacation in Spain and he was not spending much time with me. He always preferred to be with his friend. I was hurt and beginning to feel very insecure. We were going to be visiting Paris, and I was excited about showing him around, as I had been there two years before. He said he had never been there. We had been talking about it a lot. Then, one night, he suddenly told me that he *had* been there before. I asked him when, with who, etc., and he said it was with a girl he had been quite involved with before me, the only one I felt jealous about. But he always made me feel like a psycho for feeling that way. Anyway, I said, 'Why didn't you tell me you had been to Paris?' He got really mad, accused me of nagging, and started yelling that he didn't tell me because he 'knew I would react exactly like this' (jealous and insecure) and I was a 'drag.' He would rather lie to me than let me have momentary insecurity and comfort me through it. Was I completely wrong?''

Telling you what you feel is wrong

Another way some men shut a woman up is by telling her that her feelings are ''wrong'' or ''incorrect'':

''Whenever I tell him I am upset about something, if it isn't something *he* thinks is upsetting, he says, 'You shouldn't feel that way.' ''

''He says that if I feel bad about something, I should change the way I feel!''

''He tells me I must be having my period or that I need a good fuck when I get upset. He is insinuating that it can't really be me who is criticizing him; it must be due to a 'momentary female lapse of reason.' ''

Telling you you're crazy

Some men try to silence women by saying their thoughts and opinions are ''silly,'' ''crazy,'' or ''funny'' and then can't understand why a woman may raise her voice in protest:

''My boyfriend always says I'm crazy when I get riled up or sad. He thinks any woman is crazy who gets really frustrated and shows it. He doesn't even consider that there could be a valid reason for how I feel.''

''Last summer we were having one of our usual silent, nasty mornings after he had thoroughly upset, insulted, and hurt me the night before. When I finally got up to leave (I had to leave the beach because he wouldn't talk and I couldn't stand that) he ran after me and called me a 'nut-job.' "

"He has this habit of laughing or making what he thinks are witty remarks when I'm trying to talk about something serious or make a point, perhaps about politics. It makes me so angry, but if I tell him that, he asks why I'm so oversensitive. 'Don't be a baby,' he says. I can't think of anything he could do that could injure my dignity more or make me more resentful of him."

"He has started to say, 'You need help' whenever I am mad at him. The thing is, I only get really worked up into a tantrum because he won't listen to me or tries to belittle my feelings and shut me up. *That* is why I act 'crazy.' But he only sees the action, never the cause. So he says I should see a shrink and sort myself out, because it's 'obviously' nothing to do with him."

These kinds of clichéd reactions from men are emotionally violent. What is more, they carry with them the full weight of social disapproval of women's supposedly "overemotional behavior." Why do so many men still plug into these stereotypes about women or ridicule women's supposedly "hysterical" or "out-of-control" behavior?

All of these attitudes—silent indifference, ridicule, and put-downs—cut off communication in a way that is very harmful to a relationship. They have the effect of putting the man in a position of power, as he seems to be saying that he doesn't have to bother with the woman's side of the story: "Take it or leave it—I won't change." So a woman is effectively faced with the choice of fighting back, leaving, or accepting the situation.

This refusal to really listen and talk things over used to have the effect of "keeping a woman in her place" in the days when women did not have independent incomes. Although the majority still earn much less than men, now that most women do have jobs outside the home they have some possibility of leaving, and therefore more "bargaining power" and more choices in this situation.

Of course, what women really want with the men in their lives is a two-way, respectful dialogue and emotional equality, as this woman says so poignantly:

"So far I haven't found a man who was willing to stop and sit with me and say, 'You're really upset about this. What is wrong? What can I do? Tell me if I hurt you and I will try to understand.' My friends do that for me. Why can't he? It would be so wonderful to be respected like that. Even writing this makes me cry."

Some women, like this one, have found it:

"I really wonder how my fiancé managed to grow up in this culture, in this country, and be so balanced, fair, attentive and unsexist. He's not unmasculine, either. He's everything I hoped I'd find. He never lets a bad moment continue. He always addresses the conflict between us immediately and in a way that lets me know he is concerned and cares about us. He even tells me when he is angry in a respectful way. We never go to bed angry, he says life is too short for that. Of course he has his faults, but not in the areas that really matter."

And two good guys say:

"My brother is real superior with his girlfriend and it's real offensive. I wonder what he gets out of that, is that supposed to be sexy or something? If I feel like that with a girl, not equal, not open and respectful, I feel shitty."

"I'm not perfect and neither is she, but we have a lot of close times working it all out."

What Women Fight for Is Not Trivial

So this is what women in the nineties will face: as they try to make things work, humanize relationships, create more equal emotional interaction, they will encounter unconscious resistance from many men who do not see that what they are fighting to retain is not their "male pride" but their dominance. This is part of the struggle to democratize the family that women have been engaged in throughout the twentieth century. It can be so frustrating and painful at times that many women may decide not to stay in relationships—that it is too hard, too difficult and too painful to try to get men to listen and interact equally.

Indeed, the pattern of events *during* fights, once real fighting is underway, does not often encourage women to want to continue their relationships. Most women say that men continue to use the same emotionally violent tactics *during* the fight (not listening, ridiculing), that they did earlier, and many women wind up screaming or crying, feeling emotionally overwhelmed and traumatized.

Have you ever noticed any of the following infuriating tactics during a fight? If so, we hope that this analysis will help you get through them with a lot less pain.

Escalation of Fights

Refusing to see your side of things

Too many men are still trying to use clichés such as "Why don't you stop complaining?" and all the other psychological claptrap of assumed male superiority to "define" the situations and keep control of the relationship.

The I-am-right-and-you-are-wrong style during a fight is no picnic:

"His expression seems to say, Why are you behaving this way? Making a scene. I have no idea what you expect *me* to do about it."

Many men have special ways of aggravating the situation during a tense moment, by using gestures and phrases which send the message: "You are being a pain in the ass. Irrational. What do you expect me to do about *your* problem?"

"He says nothing, just looks away and shakes his head from side to side. This one movement says everything he feels: 'I can't believe you are doing this again, when will you shut up, what is your problem, what a drag, typical', etc."

"He will say 'I'm sorry *you're* upset,' in the most patronizing tone of voice, and then claim he just apologized!"

"He is very, very opinionated and his mind cannot be changed through logic, proof that he is mistaken, tears, shrieking, or anything else. Seldom is anything resolved. We don't talk anything over after a fight. We just drift back together.''

"It's always this condescending attitude of, 'Look, I know what you *think* I did, but you're wrong. I didn't do it, you're just imagining things.' Then if I insist that I know what happened, he just says, 'Look, you're wrong and I'm right. That's it. I don't want to discuss it anymore.' Sometimes I actually think I am wrong and that I made it all up."

"I get so tired at not being respected ever when I have a fight with him. He always says I'm wrong, my feelings are wrong, or even that what I'm saying he did is wrong—he didn't even *do* it. It makes me want to throw plates. Actually, what I really want to do is punch him.''

Don't forget that we are not talking about every man on the planet. But we *are* talking about a majority of men who are silencing a majority of women—women who in other parts of their lives refuse to be silenced but who have little power behind closed doors.

Compromise and trying to see another person's side of things is integral to the success of a relationship. But these noncompromising the-man-has-the-right-to-define-the-situation attitudes we are seeing here make women feel sad and alienated because a true relationship is impossible.

"My marriage was the most violent event in my life. It was short (three years) but I felt like I had lived ten years with him. We married very quickly, so I guess I never got to know him well enough. It wasn't really the lack of money or the fact that we stayed home all the time that was hard. It was the lack of understanding of my feelings that he showed. It would frustrate me so much that I would start crying and then we would have a fight because my crying pissed him off. The thing I was originally upset about would be overlooked and we would get into these violent emotional scenes about my 'weakness' and 'neediness' and his distance and criticism. It never got any further than that. We never even discussed the real problems.

"Now I am without him, and although I sometimes get sentimental and miss him, I am amazed at how peaceful my days can be. I don't have that constant feeling that a bomb is about to go off."

Laughing at you

Just as women are frequently ridiculed for bringing *up* something that bothers them, they also often experience teasing, condescending remarks from men *during* an argument. The frustration and pain women feel when they are mimicked or teased by someone they love can be devastating—and infuriating:

"I was standing there in the bathroom, crying, and he laughed at me and said, 'You really are ridiculous. Look at the facts. You're being hysterical. I've never seen such an emotional display in my life.' "

"Everything I say when we are fighting is hilarious to him. He cracks up laughing, each thing I say is funnier and more stupid than the last. You ask how I feel when this happens? Humiliated."

"He says things like, 'Oh boo-hoo-hoo, poor little girl.' I'd like to see how he'd take it if I did that to him!"

This ridicule leads some women to apologize for the fight—even when they don't want to:

"We had spent a fun day in the park sledding on the snowy hills with inner tubes from old car tires. We got home and I took a hot bath. He came in and said, 'Wasn't that fun? I'm going to give you that inner tube for your birthday.' Now I don't have a lot of money and neither did he, so I didn't want him to spend any more; I just wanted something with a little more meaning. I mean, I was twenty-eight! 'A rose would be even better,' I said. Well, it ended up being a big scene. We went out for dinner with some friends and when we came back he was sulking. He started saying that he couldn't believe I would refuse the inner tube for my birthday, that I was mercenary and ungrateful. He went on and on, cutting me off at every turn and proving how wrong each thing I said was . . . I ended up apologizing and agreeing that it had been very rude and unkind of me. I actually left that night thinking that! Then I got home and it dawned on me that I'd been wrapped around his little finger again."

Nasty fighting: going for the jugular

Often, in the last rounds of a fight, the idea isn't to air grievances and reach an understanding, but rather to wound the other person as deeply as possible:

"Lying, while fighting, is dumb, like out of anger he lied and told me he's been seeing another girl and had screwed her. I asked her name. He had to think a long time. A few months later I gently nudged her name into a conversation. He said, 'Who the hell is that? I've never heard of her!' Dummy! I feel lost when we fight. Very empty."

"If I say he hurt my feelings by not calling, he says things like, 'You might ask *yourself* why I don't call . . .' implying some vague nasty thing."

Of course, women, as well as men, can fight dirty. But men are more inclined to use any verbal weapon at hand to win, since men have been so heavily indoctrinated with the idea that a man must not let anyone step on his pride, he must never be "wrong"—"winning" is everything.

Is Going to Bed Really Making Up?

Women are often admonished not to take their fights to bed with them. After all, most of us raised, as women, with the self-concept of "pleaser"—so it would follow that we must give in where the bedroom is involved. If a woman does go to bed with a man who refuses to discuss something that matters to her and doesn't try to understand, then isn't going to bed with him capitulating?

Most women say that it is very important to them that problems and fights are not dragged out over long periods of time—that the sooner they have talked it over, the better they feel. But what if the man refuses? Often, by the time you're getting ready for bed, tension is still hanging in the air, at least for you. Should you take the fight to bed or put it aside and not let it interfere with lovemaking? It is hard to feel like having sex when you have been disregarded and humiliated. However, many women in this situation say that they have been accused of "witholding sex" to "punish" and "manipulate" the man:

"When we fight and it gets resolved in the way where I feel heard and so does he, I am incredibly aroused and want him very much. But usually, I feel emotionally beat up (he doesn't, he got his way), and so he's very turned on. I hate going to bed with him like that. But I usually do, because I don't want to deal with what would happen if I said no. Then the fight would be re-enacted and I would be even more exhausted and humiliated. It's about self-protection."

"I connect sex with feelings. So when my feelings are hurt, I don't want sex. That seems logical to me, but I get hurt even more when I hear him tell me that it's 'just sex' and I 'shouldn't be so emotional about it.' "

Women and men may be different about, say, sex. But being different has nothing to do with being cruel and disregarding what you know the other person needs—in this case, to be valued and respected in spite of her "different" feelings.

A woman can also find herself in a position of generally not wanting sex because of unresolved quarrels which have become a pattern. Even if the disagreements are small, the failures to resolve them can mount up, and a woman may feel less and less like sex:

"A pattern has started with our fights now. They usually occur at night, just before bed. Then, after the fight, if I don't feel like sex (how could I?), he accuses me of making him pay. Then, sometimes, he'll pretend to give in and agree with me so he can get his way."

"I used to be so turned on by him when we started seeing each other, then after we got engaged and then into our first year of marriage. But we fell into a bad pattern of not resolving conflicts—I thought I knew how but it's not working, and I've noticed that now I don't get aroused and want him nearly as much. It's not that we are getting used to each other after three years, either. It's almost like I feel angry when he touches me and I know it's all those things that have built up over time."

If a woman doesn't want sex for this reason, it can become "ammunition" for a man to use to put her down again. However, reserving lovemaking is a valid way in which a woman can assert her dignity and her rights, try to be heard, and get a resolution so that she can continue the relationship as *herself.*

When It All Becomes Impossible

One woman heartbreakingly describes her sadness because of alienation from a man she dearly loves:

"I want to be close to him, but I just can't, not like it was. He doesn't understand what I'm talking about, and goes really cold when I try to insist or explain. So now I have to try and forget and give up hoping it will change. I guess I thought people do change, but I'm finding out that's not necessarily true."

In other words, these patterns of fighting leave women in a no-win situation: if they can't have a dialogue with a man, it often seems they have to either accept him and things "as is," or leave, as this woman describes:

"He never apologizes, just makes fun of me if I complain or get upset about anything. If I really insist, he just walks out. This puts me in an impossible position—what do I do, leave him? If I don't want to leave him, do I have to swallow my pride and never complain? This hurts me and affects my ability to handle the rest of my life well. (I work, etc.) Then I feel too bothered by my unreleased or untalked about feelings to focus clearly on what I am doing. But if I let it out, he looks at me as if I am a 'nagging bitch' and still won't discuss the topic. So I am at a loss as to what to do. I don't know how to relate to him and still keep my sanity—but I don't want to lose him either."

Autocratic behavior leaves only black-and-white choices; a dialogue between equals would be so much better. Many men would be surprised at how much better they would feel if they took a cue from women about this.

Living in an Emotionally Violent Atmosphere

Thus, as we said in chapter 1, one of the most common, yet unnamed causes of fights in relationships is emotional battering or emotional violence. E.V., unfortunately, is the background against which many relationships are lived. We have seen how these attitudes are built in to language and "everyday" behavior toward women, in ways which are so "small" that to bring them up might lead to being

accused of pettiness. Being placed in this frame of reference can create so much tension, defensiveness, and discomfort that it is not surprising that women struggle to
change their relationships, change the emotional dynamics,
reshape the assumptions behind men's view of them. In
fact, women are heroic in their attempts to refuse to be
silenced and stereotyped.

And they are right: all of this can be changed.

Productive Fighting:
Techniques for Staying Close

Fights like the ones we have just examined can be very
harmful to a relationship. But some fighting can lead to a
positive airing of feelings that gets things back on the right
track.

How can "discussions" (fights) be constructive? Women
often say they wish men would learn some of the more
"female" skills of expressing warmth and closeness: how to
pick up subtle clues from another person, how to be more
empathetic and involved, how to respond to a request to
talk something through. In short, women want men to
learn to love not only sexually, but also emotionally.

These are just some of the values and attitudes that
women told us they would like to see more of in men
during fights:

"Be able to tell me exactly what you are feeling, as well
as you can. And then be willing to listen without judging
what I have to say. Try to put yourself in my place if you
can."

"Never close a person off: don't refuse to talk or withdraw from a woman. It only makes things worse."

Changing the way you fight

Some women have managed to change relationships from ones in which the man was not able to discuss issues into flourishing, happy, communicative ones where both listen to each other and aim towards a common goal.

Here, they describe the change:

"I like the openness we have now—the baring of ourselves to one another. It took a few years to be able to do this. He couldn't feel enough trust to be so vulnerable, but once he saw I wouldn't use it against him later somehow, he opened up and was always 'there' for me . . . now we are very happy."

"When there is a misunderstanding between us, we keep talking until we've both had our say. This relationship means so much to both of us that we're prepared to talk things through until we're back on the right track."

Another woman chose a "militant" route; by "educating" her lover, she now has an equal and happy relationship:

"In the beginning, he wouldn't do anything to help me around the house, he was just arrogant like most men, he expected me to do everything. So I had to make a big thing of making him see my point. If there were dirty dishes on the table, or dirty ashtrays, I just refused, for about a year, to move even a dish if he didn't also move a dish. If there were phone calls to be made, I just didn't make any, unless we stood right there together and he made just as many as I did. When he stopped, I stopped.

"Now it's wonderful—he is so supportive and understanding, he helped me have a way to go back to work with the children here and he really takes a part in all the housework. My sisters have both been married twice, it never lasts more than two years or three. I keep saying, 'Wait, wait! If you keep on trying, eventually you will have something great. Don't give up! Be really militant—really.' It's a shame that women have to do this to make men see, but it's worth it when you become a team and have that closeness."

To get fighting patterns to change can be difficult, because it is, in essence, a challenge to many men's whole idea of themselves: it is asking them to change their values, their stereotypes about women. But it can happen.

The best kind of fighting ends in a resolution in which each person comes to understand the other's point of view:

"We don't fight. We resolve the problem. It feels great. We used to fight because I wanted to get every place on time, and we were always late because of him. We resolved the problem by deciding that for movies, plays, and concerts, we would be on time, because it's important. For dinner, gatherings, and parties we are more lax about arrival time. Now he only feels pressure when it's important."

"After a fight we both sit down and talk things out. We then come to an understanding and cuddle up in each other's arms and fall asleep or make love, or just lie there in the quiet and listen to each other breathe."

Some couples have consciously made an agreement to try to avoid screaming, to discuss problems honestly, politely, and with kindness:

"When we feel anger start to boil in us, we both sense it and we say to each other, 'Let's take a deep breath and try to be kind but honest.' Then we sit down or lie down and try to talk it through quietly. This way anger does get expressed, but not screeched. Screeching makes us both shut down and not hear, it is useless."

"I express pretty much everything that I feel. I always have, and although I know this is basically good, I also want to learn how to keep some things to myself and not come out with everything that happens to come to mind. Doing that can hurt people unnecessarily, and has come right back at me. The man I am dating is pretty closed, opposite to me. He is very respectful and chooses his words carefully, is always conscious about how I will feel about what he says. He has difficulty expressing 'negative' (his word) feelings, sometimes, though. I have helped him to do that, and he has helped me to bite my tongue sometimes and not blurt out the first off-the-cuff thing I think of. Our communication is what I would call 'good.' "

"We definitely have some juicy arguments sometimes, but not that often. Mostly it's just that one or the other of us gets overwhelmed by work or something. He is so wonderful when I am feeling that way—he doesn't react badly or take it personally. He usually gives me a hug and a massage or just a big, fat kiss and it makes me feel so much better. If he's being crabby, I try to do the same. Both of us can 'act up' at times, we're only human, but we try to handle it with love and caring and it really works."

4

Should You Leave the Relationship?

"I know it's terrible, and it's not working. I probably should leave, but I don't want to. I love him."

So many women, including married women, have gone through long periods of asking themselves, "Is it better to stay and try to change this relationship? Or should I leave?" In this chapter, we will go through all the questions one asks oneself when reaching this decision.

Defining the Situation: Is Yours a Borderline Case?

There are many cases in which it is clearly *imperative* for a woman to leave a relationship—for example, when her days are filled with emotional or physical violence.

But what about the borderline cases—the cases in which some things are bad and some are really good? It can be very difficult to weigh the love a woman feels against the rest of the situation. How important is happiness or stability? What exactly are the feelings? Are they: love (and which kind), hate (at times, at least), fear, fascination— even just not wanting to acknowledge defeat? How hard should one try to make it work? And is it worth it to change a relationship by trying to eliminate the bad parts —or in so doing, will you extinguish the good parts too?

This is the question for the nineties: is the relationship you are in an equitable one? Or is it exploiting you, draining you emotionally, requiring you to work too hard for it? For the past few years, since the women's movement began calling for equal rights for women in the family, critics have been counterattacking by talking about the me generation—labeling women *selfish*. The latest media hype tells women that they can't "have it all," they have to *choose* between career and family. Perhaps—yet men don't have to make this choice. Neither should women, except when caring for a newborn child—when either the woman *or* the man might stay at home. In fact, the stereotype of women staying at home with the family is a pipedream today: the great majority of women with children work outside the home. Actually, this gives a woman independence: if a relationship is not fulfilling, why should she stay in it?

One of the most common reasons for staying is "because I love him." Whether a relationship is "worth it" or not often comes down to this question: How much do you love him, and in what way? And is it enough for you?

How Happy Are You in Your Relationship?

One way to find out whether you want to leave or stay in a relationship is to take this test:

1. Make a list of the qualities you have always wanted in a man and in a relationship. Do not think of your lover, just make a list as though you had never met him.

2. Now list the qualities you want and *do* have in your relationship.

3. Make another list of what you don't want.

4. Compare the two lists.

5. Put the lists aside and ask yourself how you feel when you are about to see your lover. Are you excited? Tranquil? Nervous? Are the feelings you have when you are about to see him positive, do they enhance the quality of your life? Or are you fearful and self-critical?

6. In general, how do you feel when you walk away from him? Given that you may have had a fight, or may have had a wonderful time, you can feel different on any particular day, but in *general,* do you have a feeling of well-being, that this love is worth whatever effort you put into it, a feeling of deep belonging? Or do you feel empty, lonely, tired?

7. How do you feel when you and your lover are with your friends? Are you proud to be with him? In social situations, does he do things that make you feel secure and loved or do you feel anxious and jealous?

8. Do you feel able to talk to him about everything? Or do you feel you are walking on eggshells every time you try to bring something up?

9. Do you wonder how he feels about you or does he make it a priority that you always know?

10. Are you satisfied with your sex life together? Do you feel beautiful and desirable with him? Does he tell you or show you that he loves you often enough? Are you honest with each other about your sexuality?

11. Is it your love for him or his love for you that is giving you the most pleasure in the relationship?

In looking at your answers, do you think that you get *enough* of what you want?

What is Love?

What kind of love do you feel?

One of the most confusing parts of being in an unsatisfying involvement is trying to work out exactly *what* you feel for your partner.

There are so many different kinds of love. One kind— the feeling of being "in love"—is a true part of the joy of being alive, luscious, exhilarating, unbounded:

"The first time I went to bed with him, I felt as though the world had stopped and I was a shooting star sending out enough light to illuminate the blackest of black holes. Both in bed and out, it was an overpowering sensation and I couldn't get enough of him.''

"When I first saw him I felt a lurch, a leap, and then a kind of internal sigh, an, 'At last. Where have you been for so long?' A deep sense of recognition. It also felt scary as hell. He was like everyone I'd ever been in love with before in some small way and then himself, more so. He is beautiful to look at, astoundingly intelligent, very warm and beautifully sensual (but only in bed, almost never in public), his voice makes my ears feel good and my chest and spine, he has very penetrating eyes, his sense of humor is delightful, he can do or figure out almost anything, and he's maddening, frustrating, infuriating, invigorating, unpredictable, uncontrollable, and nice.''

"Both times I have been in love I've known it at once. The usual chatter that goes on in your head—which you more or less think of as yourself—suddenly seems much fainter and smaller, and underneath is something larger, quieter, more sure of itself.''

Some women don't think it is worth staying in a relationship without this kind of love. As one woman puts it:

"I can't imagine not loving totally. With abandon. It would be like being half alive. Not really getting all you deserve. It would be a rip-off!''

Is love caring or passion?

But other women distrust this kind of love and don't want to be in a relationship in which they are deeply "in love." They don't like the feeling of being out of control, the roller coaster ups and downs. They find it all too painful and overwhelming—much too volatile and dangerous for true happiness:

"Being in love can give pleasure, even joy, but most of the time it's painful, unreal, and uncertain. It took a long time to learn anything from it, and most of what I learned is that I should avoid it."

"I do not like being in love. I feel too vulnerable. I would rather be with someone I feel comfortable and safe with than be in love."

But in the end, why make judgments? All the forms of love are valid; which we prefer depends on what we want from a relationship at a given time in our lives. "Settling" is an unsettling word; choosing to be with someone who has, say, half of the qualities you want can be seen as accepting—truly loving someone with and in spite of flaws.

Interestingly, while people usually say there are only two different types of love—being passionately "in love," or being nurturing and caring (usually, learning to care over time)—generally, women's descriptions of their feelings do not exactly fit these neat categories. Most women say that passion, or passionate love, means feeling not only physical passion but also emotional passion, and often they say that one cannot exist without the other. The body-mind split that is so prevalent in Western society is not one that usually emerges in women's descriptions of the feelings they call love.

It's nice to also hear some of the good guys define what love means to them:*

* From *The Hite Report On Male Sexuality*, Alfred A. Knopf, 1981.

"I fell in love with my wife when I was seventeen. It was exciting. It made life beautiful. It made me feel like Superman."

"The air did breathe her scent and her touch was tattooed on my flesh and her warmth was near. The roses did give off more scents and the magic innocence of youth was everywhere and the world was at peace."

"I felt wonderful. There are no words for it. I went around for weeks and months seeing the world as a place of beauty and hope, rather than ugliness and despair. I spent hours being enchanted by the presence of the woman. Every little nook and cranny of my head was comprehended fully and cherished for the first time in my life."

Another man describes how uncomfortable love makes him:

"I've fallen in love four times. It's exactly the feeling of fear—the pang in the solar plexus. And the other symptoms are the same—the giddy disorientation, the shaky hands, the wild surmises. But what does it mean if, basically, one's *body* responds to dread and to 'falling in love' the same way? And why do we prettify this?"

Other good guys describe frustration with the way they were raised to think about love, saying that it holds them back:

"Dad's idea of a man was someone who hunted, fished, played sports, etc. Love was not to be taken seriously or given free rein in your life."

"I do not fall in love very easily. I am very defensive about my freedom and really fight my feelings when I feel like I may be falling in love. This is something I would sort of like to change. I want to express it more than I can now. I have nothing against being in love, I am just not looking for a long-term commitment. I guess this is why my mind will not let me be in love as much as I sometimes want to be."

Is not "loving enough" a reason to leave?

Some women carry a secret guilt for not being enough in love with their mates, not "wildly in love":

"What about when he loves you—you know he loves you, even though he may not give you just what you want —what then? Should you leave? Do you have the right to leave? He hasn't done anything wrong, after all."

What if you don't love him enough (how much is that)?

"I have found a man who gives me all the love, nurturing, etc. that I always wanted, but he's not a 'bad boy' like the previous ones. I don't know if you understand what I mean. But this results in my not having the same kind of wild passion for him like I did with other men. I sometimes wonder if I should stay in this relationship if I don't have a crazy and passionate feeling towards him. This love isn't 'less' though, it's just different."

"I'm seeing a nice guy who is sweet and loyal. It's very undramatic and nothing ever really happens. I am bored, although I feel bad saying so. Although there are none of those gross ups and downs I had when I was married to M., this is too much the reverse. It doesn't feel good; I thought it would be the solution, to find someone I could grow to love, but it's unsatisfying."

One woman celebrates leaving a boring, unfulfilling marriage:

"I can't believe I spent all that time in a marriage that was so empty. I never had fun with my husband. I never knew you could have fun with a man! Now I know I'm wrong, my lover and I have a riot together. We spend a lot of time in bed, talking and enjoying each other's bodies. He really appreciates me and shows me in lots of ways. I'm so glad I found this and didn't spend my whole life lonely in a marriage bed."

Another enjoys the "realness" of her imperfect one:

"He's a lot of things that I didn't think I would choose, or stand for. He's very right-wing, conservative, bigoted, laid back, unfashionable, uneducated, and unliterate. But he's also warm, funny, affectionate, consistent, loyal, appreciative, sexy, big, a great lover, a jock, passionate, conscious, adoring, kind, generous, protective, and an absolute darling."

Pressure to give more than you've got

Another feeling women sometimes describe is living with the vague feeling of not giving enough, a feeling of semidisapproval or disappointment coming from the man, who feels he is not getting enough attention, that the woman never has enough time for him. It is interesting to hear from these women because this problem is usually one that men complain of!

One woman answered this unspoken accusation in the following way:

"You are assuming my function is to serve you—and therefore always have a vague bitchy attitude or pout when I'm doing something else—even when I'm working! *Especially* when I'm working! You think all my time and attention should be focused on *you!*"

Are you criticized, or criticizing yourself, for not spending enough time with him? So many women have full-time jobs that one of the most pressing concerns women face now is how to deal with the assumption that women should always be there for men. Most men turn to women for comfort and attention, to make life civilized: they believe we should dress nicely for them, listen to them, be ready to go out with them whenever they want. (Was life ever like that, given the enormous amount of work women have always done in the home?) Today it is impossible for a woman to be a full-time support person, plus carry on a career, raise children—and do they want to? Especially for someone who does not reciprocate that support?

"Before I started this job I had a very light schedule workwise and usually had a couple of hours to fool around at home in the afternoons, fixing the place up and stuff. In the beginning it's so much fun to fuss over your nest, especially when he really appreciates it.

"But I got this job in '88 and it's a job I'd been trying to get for six years. Sure, he was very happy for me, and we planned all the things we could do with this extra money.

"But when things started getting busy and I started coming home at 6:30 or 7:00, obviously the house didn't look so good and neither did I! And I didn't feel like having sex sometimes or entertaining him in some other way (dinner, etc.). This is still a problem and he acts sort of stunned that I am not keeping everything nice and pretty and delicious and perfumed for him. I end up feeling he has a free-floating dissatisfaction and anger from this which makes me nervous and resentful in return."

Unequal emotional support

We have seen how a lot of women are doing the emotional upkeep in a relationship. Many women are trained to please others, men in particular. Do you find yourself constantly worrying about pleasing your partner? One woman describes this state of mind:

"I like him, but I also like to have time alone, sometimes I like to sleep alone—not feel pressured to be 'sexy' or ready for sex when he wants it, to be friendly and charming. There are a lot of nights when I come home from work so wiped out that the thought of sex just doesn't interest me, but I have it anyway, because I don't want to make him think I don't find him attractive. I know he doesn't concern himself with the same worries—if he doesn't want sex, wants to lie around and look like shit, he doesn't worry about me."

We can become so involved with trying to figure out how to please, or make the other person emotionally comfortable, that we forget to watch out for our own needs. We think, "How much can I give?," not, "I need him to nurture my resources so I can reach the goals I have set for myself." We are accustomed to putting men first.

Thinking it through

Usually there is no one incident that tells a woman she had better get out of a relationship; more often it is a series of incidents, a constant feeling of being emotionally in suspense, or the same serious problems recurring. But as these kinds of relationships gradually take their toll, battering and eroding your morale, it is easy to lose touch with how much it is really costing to continue, and make the wrong decision:

"I once heard that the definition of insanity was to keep doing the same thing over and over again and expect different results. That was the story of this last relationship."

Married women often spend several years of anguish debating whether to leave a marriage before deciding to get a divorce; they later say, on the whole, that they were far more unhappy during this period of trying to decide than during or after the divorce.

Agonizing Choices: When It's Really Fifty-Fifty

In the same way, women in half-good half-bad relationships can go through utter agony trying to work out what to do:

"Some days I think I can't go on one more minute, I feel so sad. And other days I can't imagine leaving him, I love him so much. I always love him, but sometimes I wonder if that is enough."

"He has never done one big thing, like sleep with someone else or forget my birthday or something. It's just all these 'little' things, always this feeling of waiting for the other shoe to drop, never knowing what kind of a day we will have together. I don't know whether I love him or not anymore. I just don't know.''

"When we started having scenes and I realized that I was crying two or three times a week because of fights we had, I remember thinking, 'Why am I staying?' But I loved so much about him and my feelings went so deep that I couldn't leave just because things were rough. I had to wean myself away very gradually.''

"When he does something nice, I think, 'See, he really does care, we really are in love, everything's really fine, remember this the next time things go wrong with him.' And then the next day, when he does something really mean and rotten, I think, 'This is how it *really* is, most of the time.' And I know that it's true. I wonder what I should do at this point.''

"I knew when we fell in love that we would not have a smooth relationship, because he is a very temperamental man. But I'm not the kind of person who needs to 'conform,' or have a 'model home' type of relationship. So it didn't bother me. At least it didn't used to. But I can't quite think of one reason that I should stay in this relationship. On the other hand, I can't really bring myself to break it off, even though everything that is going on right now is goddamned awful.''

Borderline good-bad relationships are hard to work out. Part of you may say, "No matter what, no matter how bad it is, the feeling that he *does* want me, he *does* love me, is so strong that I can't be wrong!" The belief in this feeling, or the memory of it—even just the longing for that feeling—

is hard to resist. Especially when your self-esteem is wilting from bad treatment. So, the worse things get, the harder it becomes to give up the belief that "underneath it all, he loves me. He says so, I know it's so, and he will come through, just as soon as he's over this difficult period."

He may indeed love you *in his way.* But if this relationship is continually disappointing you or hurting you, then what can you do? In most cases, it is better to leave, unless some drastic changes can be made.

One of the best ways to think clearly is to spend a week or two alone, away from him, reorienting your life—seeing friends or working on projects you especially like. After initial cramps of pain, you will find your equilibrium returns and you can begin to think more clearly about what should be done.

How hard is it to tell him you want to get away and have time alone? It can be very difficult because you may fear his reaction, and, on a deeper level, you may hate giving up his love. However unsatisfying your relationship may be, there are probably times when the love is (or was) great; the memory of that can make it difficult to accept that the "bad" part is, and will continue to be, the reality.

Even harder to give up than his love for you may be your love for him. Leaving him doesn't necessarily mean you must stop loving him and won't miss him. Obviously no one can stop loving someone in one minute. But as well as being sad, you probably feel a lot of anger at things that have happened. Acknowledging your anger is crucial; it is a key that can unlock hidden strength and great inner resources. Feminists and some psychologists consistently point out how much of women's depression (for which we are prescribed a great deal of medication and therapy) is anger turned inward. It becomes turned inward because we ladies aren't supposed to exhibit that "male," "aggressive," "bad," "unpleasant" feeling! But there is no better time for remembering our reasons for anger than during the depressed and agonizing moments of contemplating breaking off or radically redefining a relationship.

The Stages of Leaving

The leave-taking process (whether literally or just in your heart) usually happens in stages. First, women bargain with themselves: "OK, so I won't ask him to do the laundry or the dishes anymore—it's not worth it. I love him, he's a man, and you just can't expect this overnight, but I can enjoy him—and where else could I find a better lover or a man who loves me this much?" When this bargain doesn't really work, next to go is a woman's belief that she *is* loved. Still, she may stay because, "I still love how well we know each other, what we have built up over time, and I hope he believes in this too. . . ." and so on.

With each bargaining chip in this interior dialogue a woman gives up more and more of her dreams, and denies more and more of her needs, until she feels very emotionally alone. As she struggles she may feel she is giving more than he is, trying harder to make it work:

"Why doesn't he seem to want to meet me half way? Does he even understand that he is not? Will the relationship ever be better? Am I a fool to continue it? Should I keep on struggling? Give less energy to it? Should I *leave?*"

Double lives: leaving emotionally

In order to deal with unsatisfactory or half-satisfactory relationships, many women lead double lives emotionally, staying in their relationship but limiting the part of themselves they risk exposing to their lover. They find they channel more and more of their emotional energy into friends, children, and their work:

"I just don't focus so much on it anymore. Then if I'm disappointed, it doesn't matter so much. Maybe the love will build back, but if not, it's better to have other parts of my life that I'm involved in. Then everything goes smoother."

"When I got married I thought we'd want to be together all the time, else I couldn't see getting married. But I've changed, now I don't fool myself that things will ever be that way. Other things take up my time now: children and community."

"My business gives me more consistent satisfaction than my marriage."

Most women separate themselves emotionally in these cases without really ever trying; it just happens. They find themselves drifting away, no longer able to relate so fully to the other person who does not seem to see what is happening. They find they are not as close as before, that they automatically hold part of themselves back. As one woman describes it:

"The relationship doesn't mean as much as it once did. It's peripheral to my life now, because I have grown and changed and he has not."

This emotional alienation can also express itself sexually. If a woman is offering her real self and her true feelings, and is constantly hurt, a pattern will usually be established:

she gradually wants sex less and less as she becomes less emotionally involved in the relationship. Often, at this point, the man starts to complain that there is not enough sex and may begin looking elsewhere. Sound familiar? This leads to further distance and alienation (which the woman may struggle at times to break through, as seen in chapter 3).

When women leave sexually and emotionally, without actually removing themselves from the scene, the question they often ask is, "Do I want to stay in this relationship and compromise, accept getting less out of it than I want, the kind of love I dreamed of, or should I leave and begin my life again?"

Quite a few delay leaving, because they doubt whether another relationship would be different:

"My kid is twelve and having a lot of problems adjusting to life without his dad. I know it's better for both of us this way, but things happen that make me wonder. Like the other night, my boyfriend started accusing me of coming on to a man I work with. It's not true. It turned into a silly fight that ended up nowhere. My son was watching from the stairs and got all upset and started crying. It reminded him of me and his dad. Eventually I got him tucked in, and John and I went to bed in silence. I lay there and thought, 'You thought it would be different after you divorced Dan, but the same thing is happening now. Is it you? Why is this happening? It wasn't this way in the beginning.' "

Other women delay leaving because they don't want to go through the pain:

"I know that this affair isn't making me happy, but I just can't bear to go through the pain again of separating my life from someone, of starting over. My divorce was so hard, and I just don't want to do it again. Even though I'm not feeling fulfilled, I think it might be less painful to stay than to leave."

And still others (mostly with children) stay simply for financial reasons:

"We got pregnant and married early and I never really developed a means of providing for myself, you know. Now the fact that he supports me is the only reason I stay. The love is gone. People say I should leave, and I wish I could, but with what?"

Statistically speaking, 50 percent of marriages end in divorce, and most of these divorces are initiated by women. Just as many women with very little money leave their marriages as women with more money. Therefore, most women today clearly are ready to take on extra jobs and face whatever sacrifices are necessary, rather than stay in bad relationships.

When you leave, even though you still love him

Leaving is never easy. Listen to one woman's decision to force herself to stay away and what her reasons are:

"What is there to do? Last night, while I was out, my 'friend' (my lover) called, very distressed, apparently, about the distance that has developed between us. I am distressed too. But the closeness of the relationship would only be possible for me if he was to change. If I would try to carry the relationship, accepting him as he is, I would explode with indignation, take revenge on him for everything that I had accepted in demure affection for the sake of the truly wonderful moments we are able to share. That way I would eventually kill the potential of these moments happening between us. Then I would have to withdraw because there would be nothing to stay for. So, to preserve what I love I must withdraw now.

"I must withdraw for the sake of my belief in a real—or what I call real—relationship, because I must grow more and more to become myself, to be able to respond to other people with all my potential, if I want to have a chance to meet the person with equality—if ever I should meet the person with whom it is possible to fulfill my belief. I believe you have to learn to treasure all you have and not go beyond the line of what you honestly can treasure. If that means that I have to live more remote from another human being than I wish to do, then that is the better pain to take into the future."

And two others:

"I look at him across a crowded room or in the cab that he drives and I see such beauty, a man I love so much. But the things he says to me, the criticisms and denegration of my character and integrity are taking their toll. I just can't pretend that I am happy anymore. I'm so tired. It's a constant, incessant disappointment—I *live* in disappointment. It's crushing my optimism and hope about life. I have to leave, but the thought terrifies me. I wish so much that it could be what I thought, and what I wanted it to be."

"I didn't realize how this was affecting me—I haven't been aware of the way it has eroded my sense of self and my attitude towards life. But I have been doing a lot of talking with my friends, and now I know I have to make the break. It's going to be hard. But I can't do anything else, he won't change, he's told me so."

Some of the saddest statements come from women who are saying good-bye to those they love. Listen to this woman's letter to the man she was leaving:

"I love you so much. Our problem has nothing to do with my friends, as you claim. You are so proud and try to make me feel so lousy that I don't want to share them with you. You want me to be just like Jean, someone who grimaces when asked if she is still with Jim—someone who allows for so much hurt and being walked on so much— you think that's a wonderful woman. Well, that is a wonderful woman (there are many things I like about her), but that's a stupid woman too. If you think that's what a relationship should be, then we have very different ideas about that.

"I tried every way I know to be everything I wanted to be for you, and it hasn't been enough. I have a body and a brain many men would love to have as their own, but you reject them time and time again, while lusting after or making passes at God knows who (plus one of my dearest friends). I feel many conflicting emotions about it, but mostly I wonder, *why?* I've always been there for you, loving you, loving your brain, loving your cock, caring and trying to help you and myself be the best we can be together. Trying to hold the team together. But I can't do it alone. I can't live with you, knowing things go on, like your making a play for Laura after I've gone to work. I mean, what is the *reason?* I have been trying to fulfill you for eighteen months and I feel like I'm bruised and battered from being for our team all alone and beating my head against a brick wall.

"I love you desperately, but there is nothing I can do anymore except drown with you, or take some action. I need to be loved, wanted, to know someone really thinks I'm gorgeous sometimes, who gives me his undivided attention sometimes. I've lost all that feeling with you, and I need it desperately. You must realize how you need it too, and then see how I do. You require so much sexual attention that having a woman (whom others would want) living with you and delighting so excessively in your boner isn't even enough for you! You require so much emotional attention that your friends have to make up for all the love and attention you seem to need from me and don't think you're getting! Christ! Then I am chastized for crying in the mornings and dreaming of evenings with you when you ravage me and we eat dinner and completely lose ourselves in each other. How can you reprimand me for wanting that? My God, are you a fool? That is the *best!* Don't you remember?

"There is no law written that that has to end. And there's no reason why I should be told that I'm a pessimist and a fatalist if I say I don't think it will ever come again. Because I *do* believe it should, but I don't believe you can right now. Or you won't.

"So let me go—love me enough to set me free from this thing and live while you work it out. I love you and want to feel that that is something you treasure again. Until then, I have to keep it inside because I can't give it to you anymore. Not until you really want it—in the right way — and are willing and able to grab it by the balls with me and do it."

Are you afraid to leave?

If you are in a bad relationship and don't want to leave, ask yourself: why? Clarify your thoughts by making a list of what you are getting out of it. Is he interesting? Sexy?

Sometimes very understanding? Make a list of your fears, too.

Are any of the following your reasons for staying?

- I won't find anyone else.
- I won't find anyone else as good, interesting, sexy, etc.
- He's more special than anyone I've ever met. (Why?)
- This is my last chance because of my age.
- I've already invested so much time, I can't give up now.
- I don't think people should leave other people.
- He says he loves me, and even though he acts appall-ingly sometimes, I believe him. I feel it is true.
- His love is more important to me than any other love could be because _____.
- I like the social approval of having a partner.
- I don't like being "single."
- I made a commitment.

If you answer yes to any of the above, you need not be too hard on yourself. Still, ask yourself whether you have become debilitated, unable to judge your own situation, and not strong enough to look for a way to get your own needs met. Are you always putting your own needs on the back burner, while things get "straightened out," or you "help him"? The imbalance of power many men set up in relationships typically leads women to ask themselves, "Is he feeling all right? Does he still love me? What is his mood today?" not, "Do I feel all right? Do I want this kind of relationship?"

One woman recalls her own experience of not being strong enough to leave, to take her own needs seriously enough:

"I spent a year with him. For three quarters of that year I was unhappy. For a while I was willing to put up with the sadness because he meant so much to me. But I didn't keep in touch with my friends. I was sloppy at work, and my health suffered. I was lucky enough to have good friends who were careful to be supportive of my desire to be with him and at the same time gently showed me that my life and my own sense of self-worth were being decimated by the relationship. I got to the point where I was ready to consider their side of things, where I was ready to see that the good no longer outweighed the bad. What I was getting from the relationship was not enough to compensate for the amount that was being taken from me.

"I left, but it was premature. I wasn't ready to let go of him. I still saw some value in what we shared together, and couldn't bear never to see him again. So, after a couple of weeks of incessant calling and visiting from him, I gave in and went back. Six months later, the problems were even worse than the last time.

"Finally, I had had it. I spent a couple of months talking about it to my friends, about what kind of relationship I wanted and what kind of relationship I was in—and the incongruity between the two. I realized that he would never change in the ways I needed him to (even having let go of some of my less important needs, I still knew this would be true about the remaining ones), and I could not be happy in the relationship the way it was.

"That winter was very hard. I really never thought I would be able to leave, I didn't think I could bear the pain, couldn't stand to think about being without him, him being with someone else, me being with someone else, all those thoughts. But I drew on the strength of my friends and what I knew in my heart of hearts was right for me. I couldn't compromise myself anymore, couldn't stand to watch myself disappear any longer. So I left."

Making the Break

There comes a point at which many women can no longer deny the overwhelming need they have to get out of a relationship—no matter how hard this may be psychologically, financially, or socially.

These women explain what helped them make the decision to leave:

"I was told to try making a list of all the pros and cons. I resented this, I thought it was unromantic and too practical, like buying a car, but I was so unhappy I had to do something. So I tried and it really helped. I made a list of the good things with us, and the bad things. Then I made a list of what I really wanted and a list of what I was getting. When I saw it on paper, and it wasn't running around in my head, all jumbled up, I was able to think more clearly and make a decision."

"I bounced everything off my two best friends, a woman and a man. I had bottled things up for so long, so this helped me in two ways: I got things said, and I got their advice. I crossed a line doing this, like I was not 'his' anymore."

"I gave up trying to talk to *him* about it and started talking to *others* about it. My male friends were a real big help, you know, because they are the kind of guys I would like my lover to be. I asked them about the way they treat their women as lovers, the way they speak to them and things they do for them, and ways they love them. And the answers almost broke my heart because they said all the things of my dreams, you know, like what I always wanted to hear him say but never did. I had repressed those desires so as not to be let down. Hearing them from my friends gave me a strong dose of reality, the *bad* reality of my relationship."

"I filled my life up with other things, starting small and building up. I didn't want to, like I wanted to just lie around and wait for his call to tell me whether we were going to do anything that night, (week, year!), waiting on him to 'come through.' So instead, I made other plans, saw movies and friends. I even flirted a little! After a few months of this, I realized I could live without him. I became detached, sort of."

Leaving with the Least Pain

One day at a time

The concept of "one day at a time" has helped a lot of people get over various problems with drugs, alcohol, food, money, gambling, sex, and people. This credo also works very well when breaking up with someone, because there will be a "hole" inside you at first. If you think about having to live with that hole "forever," chances are it will seem too overwhelming, and you may not go through with it. The real truth is that the hole will *not* be there forever, but that's so hard to believe or even conceive of when you are hurting. *But it is true.* So, to make the pain of loss more "manageable," think only of today, not yesterday or tomorrow. It is remarkable how quickly you will find the days add up, and the healing *will* come. As one woman said:

"At first I worried, if I leave, will I really have something better? I really didn't believe I would. I learned, after time, that the answer was, 'Yes! Myself! I will have myself back!' "

Most women say the worst part is *before* they make the decision to leave; after that it is much easier. And one *does* get beyond the feelings:

"When someone told me then that one day I would say 'John who?' I thought they were crazy and shallow. I thought they didn't know a thing about love, about passion, about pain. But they were right. Today I feel completely secure in my decision to leave, feel no regret, only gratitude to myself for realizing I wasn't getting my needs met and doing something about it, and to my friends for helping me through it."

Don't talk to your ex

Many women say that the way to leave is to have absolutely *no* contact with their ex-lovers whatsoever. This may seem extreme or overly dramatic, but it isn't.

Immediately after you've summoned up enough strength and courage to leave, you usually feel very vulnerable. There is a fragile side to every person that is naturally heightened at a time of wrenching away from a lover, no matter what has transpired. As these women put it:

"Your emotions are enlarged and sometimes seem crazy. When I was leaving him, I would sentimentalize him, and then get into huge fights with people on the subway every morning. I'd yell and even push them. My rage came out at them instead of him—I was so devastated I hardly knew what I was doing."

"It's as if you're a walking wound, and anything that happens can feel like salt thrown at you, even if someone on the street is mean or something. Things that normally would just irritate you are suddenly absolutely horrible."

This is by no means meant as a definition of women as wounded victims all by themselves; breaking up is also a painful and vulnerable experience for many men, as this man describes movingly:

"It was the only time in my life that I ever cried myself to sleep at night and I did this frequently. I did not actually consciously think about suicide but I considered myself already dead. A greater emptiness and sense of loss I have not known. Since that time I have not been able to love a woman with such utter abandonment of my feelings; I just haven't been able to do it. I still feel the pain. I know if I were to see her right now I know my heart would jump into my throat."

Seeing a person you are trying to leave only adds to your sadness. The point is to treat yourself especially well when you are breaking up, and not to get impatient with yourself for being emotional. It is only natural.

"Don't talk to your ex-lover" includes the following:

- Not reading letters, old ones or new ones.
- Not answering phone calls. A phone call or a letter from the person you are leaving will probably only make you feel even less happy, less convinced of your own decision, and less able to stick to your priorities.

- If flowers come, throw them out or give them to someone.
- Give all your photographs to a friend for safekeeping. They might be fun to have someday, but right now they are an emotional mine field that you don't need to negotiate.
- Ask friends you have in common not to mention your old love to you if they can help it, and don't indulge your own curiosity. Knowing where he was last night, or who he was with, will probably only be upsetting.
- Avoid going to old haunts or that favorite restaurant. Promise yourself you can go back in a year; by then you may not want to!
- On special anniversaries, like the first time you slept with him, make plans to be with very good friends—or even your new lover!

Realize that this is only limiting your life for a little while. It is not a permanent situation. These feelings *are* going to pass, even though you may feel they won't. And your life will again be your own; you will again take charge.

Go out with someone else?

Even though it might be the last thing in the world you feel like doing, it could be helpful to go out on a few dates, as this woman found:

"The idea of going out on a date when I left him made my stomach turn. The idea of *men* made my stomach turn. I couldn't even think of kissing one. But my girlfriend said, 'I know you don't want to do this, but go out with John tonight.' She got me dressed up and did my face and I went. And I had a terrific time. I didn't kiss him or anything, but for five hours I got a lot of great attention, and it soothed my bruised ego and heart and did more for me than anything else."

See your women friends

When you are exhausted from trying to make a relationship with a man work and think nothing can make you feel better, it's amazing how energizing it can be to get together with your women friends (see also chapter 7).

"After I broke up with him, I asked all my women friends over to dinner. We ate like pigs, drank champagne, laughed, cried, and it was one of the best nights of my life. They helped me get through so much, I wanted to thank them."

"Women are the most important people in my life. My close relationships with women have kept me going when all else failed."

"My best friend has helped me go through childbirth, divorce, depression. Every time I've needed a helping hand, she's been there."

Recognizing Your Anger

An important part of leaving and being able to say goodbye to all the feelings is to recognize and express not only sadness (if you are sad) but also anger. Whether you decide to express this anger with the man in question, or with a friend or counselor, this will help keep the anger from turning around on you and making you feel confused, guilty, depressed, or "worthless."

Anger is not a "bad" emotion; however, as we have said, it is one that women are so often told they mustn't feel, or God forbid, display. It is "unladylike"—men reserve that right. But we *do* have the right, and it is important to acknowledge it, to *say* that we have not been treated well when we haven't.

One woman describes this very clearly:

"By the end my anger became a source of strength for me. Realizing it and holding on to it was one of the most empowering feelings I ever had. You always learn that 'ladies shouldn't get angry,' and 'if you can't say something nice about [to] someone, say nothing at all.' Well, that's crap. When I was able to really realize the anger I felt towards him, I was able to express it to myself and friends and this propelled me through leaving him. When I felt myself beginning to weaken, I would tap into it and it gave me hope, energy, and determination about the change I was making."

Using the Break as a Major Opportunity

Most women feel very good after finally making the break, as this woman describes:

"I spent the second year we were together living in the past, remembering how good it was in the beginning.

Things were going really badly, he became very cold and distant. On one occasion I planned a lovely second-anniversary dinner for us, spent all day running around looking for just the right kind of steak, the best wine, the perfect candles, and he never turned up! He was busy getting a tan at the beach. That night I lay in bed trying to sleep and remembering how he used to say to me, 'I'm so in love with you, I can hardly eat!'

"The final break came after one morning when I dropped by his apartment on the way to work with a bunch of flowers, and he was in bed with someone. I threw the keys down on the bed and walked out.

"I spent the next two weeks at a friend's house, someone he had never met. I holed up there and spent time with her and other friends, keeping away from him. His best friend had a spare key, and, while he was away one weekend, I went in and got all my things.

"Leaving him was the best thing I ever did. I was unhappy for so much of the time I was with him, and didn't realize (or forgot!) that life can be so much better than that. I had forgotten how to laugh, how to wake up on a Saturday morning and look forward to the weekend, alone, with friends or family. Now I laugh, and look forward to coming home to my warm apartment, doing nice things for myself, traveling, going out on dates—I feel I have sprouted wings. I own myself again."

All the things you never had time for, were too depressed to do or always meant to do "when you had time," do now! They can be small things: taking bubble baths, buying makeup, working out, taking yourself to the movies, getting lots of sleep, renting a funny video (chances are you have not laughed much lately). Or, it can mean starting a major new project, a job search, or a serious hobby that you have been putting off but have dreamed of for half your life. Take steps now and do it.

Changing your life, reorienting your life—what a great opportunity! You can do *anything.* How many times are there in life when you can be so free, have so many options? You have "lost" something, but you have also gained. You have got *yourself* back, you have a chance to review all parts of your life. Do you like your job? Where you live? Your friends? What major goals in life have you put aside? Use this time to your advantage. Explore the world! Reinvent things for yourself in daring new ways! You'll never regret it.

5

The Good Stuff

After all this, you may be wondering if there is anything good left. Well, yes there is!

Do you have a right to enjoy the good stuff and be "in love" even if your relationship isn't perfect or if there are terrible problems?

Women are generally thought to be "masochists" if they are in a problematic relationship. The atmosphere of social disapproval is so heavy that many women harbor a secret fear that "I shouldn't really be enjoying this—he screamed at me yesterday and said the most disgusting things. No woman in her right mind should be treated that way. If I let myself enjoy these kisses he is offering me now, it must mean that I accept the relationship, including the insults. But I *do* like what he is doing now. Am I hopeless? Is this a loss of my integrity?"

Celebrating the Great Times

Most of us can think of great times we have had in our relationships, or particular ways of spending time with those we love, moods that are happy and very precious:

"You know what I like? I like noodling around the house in my oldest clothes on a Saturday morning, talking with him in our 'language,' with him in his old clothes too, or his ancient terry-cloth bathrobe, gradually waking up, looking in the refrigerator, picking up last night's dishes, looking out the window, deciding if we want to take the dogs out for a walk."

"When I wash my hair, it takes forever. Sometimes he keeps me company while I do it, or shampoos it for me— how I love that! Then he sits and talks to me while I dry it. What a doll."

"I love weekends when we never get out of bed for a whole day. We wake up and make love. Then we eat breakfast, watch a movie, and go back to bed. All afternoon, we watch TV, snack, make love and nap. It's best when it's raining outside. We unplug the phone and disappear from the world together."

"I love going out with him. He's fun. When he calls and says he's coming over, I get butterflies, he's so exciting. I get dressed thinking about how he'll react when he sees me, thinking how he will like how I look. When he comes in the door, he *always* smiles, hugs and kisses me. I love the smell of his leather jacket mixed with his cologne as he presses against me. Then we usually take a cab and go out to eat. He holds my hand and kisses me during dinner. I'm so happy—this has been going on for SIX MONTHS!"

"I like to shower with him and watch the water fall along his strong legs and across his shoulders, watch him lather soap all over his hairy chest and arms and his penis. Sometimes I give him oral sex under the hot water! He loves to do the same to me, or sometimes he bathes me in the tub with bubbles and masturbates me. I could keep that up for hours. I usually come two or three times. Sometimes we get so wild that our legs are weak and we can hardly get out of the bathroom!"

"We've been together four years and have a terrific life. After a long work week, (I suppose we could both be called workaholics) we jump in the old Karmann Ghia and speed out to our beach cottage. We have made a lot of friends out here over the years, and it's so peaceful and calming that we never want to go back home on Sundays. People out here talk about birds, development, church, tides, babies. It's beautiful. It's good for us, our antidote. We make love out here under the stars in the summer, in front of the fire in the winter. I make roast beef for Sunday lunch. Oh, I love our life."

"I was getting really sick of answering these questions up till now because it bugged me to look at some of the things that aren't perfect in our marriage, like I was misrepresenting. But now I see some things I didn't see before—*and* I can tell you about the happiness and excitement I feel about him (after eleven years!) He travels a lot so I spend time on my own at our house, but I see lots of friends and have fun. I always miss him badly, though, so the best part about his traveling is when I know he is coming home and I prepare some delicious food and take a long bath and shave my legs and dress up and light the candles. It honestly feels like a first date to both of us."

"I can be scrambling over stones to cross a river or climbing up some beach cliffs and feel totally at peace with him and myself and the world around me. I can feel how he is in the same trance of peace and contentment in the way he notices with loving interest little happenings in the water or amongst the grass."

Are these the same women we heard from in chapter 1? How can they sound so different?

The men women describe here are, indeed, the men that at other times are distant and silent or exhibit other "male" distancing patterns discussed earlier. Most relationships are mixed; there are the good parts and the not-so-good parts. Even though women may be having the problems we saw earlier in the book, most also find many things they cherish and enjoy in their relationships. It's not only women, but men, too, who repeatedly describe feeling joy and the essence of being alive when they are in love, as we see here in these men:

"Every once in a while there is that strange, almost overpowering feeling that makes you want to be with a person all the time—through good and bad—just because it is inside you."

"I don't know how to tell you what it felt like except to say that to find the existence of another person who was dear to me reawoke a long-buried joy for life and the desire to give myself to whatever life, through her, had to offer."

"The time I fell most deeply in love . . . I couldn't sit still, I jumped up and down and danced, I felt like running places instead of walking, I looked in the mirror and laughed with glee, my heart pounded and I couldn't breathe, I wanted to let everyone know. I wanted to give. I wanted to share. I wanted to tell all the lonely people to hang in there, it would be along. Then sometimes I could just sit for hours and thank God for putting this person in my life. I always had the feeling that something in the universe had clicked when I met this person—that for some beautiful reason we were together. It's an honor and a privilege to be in love. It demands my honesty and courage. Above all it's a time of soul-searching, a type of respect and I have to stand face-to-face with my own selfishness, anger, false pride, and just make sure I don't fuck anyone over, I don't hurt me or her."

How Not to Feel Guilty for "Compromising"

Perhaps you only enjoy the sex and affection but little else in your relationship. Maybe you think he's a great guy, but he really doesn't have a clue about you—or how to have an equal relationship with a woman. Maybe you really like the places he finds for you to go together, but you find it hard to talk to him (at least, much harder than talking to your woman friends).

Does this mean that you have hidden, nefarious motives for being in the relationship? Are you just bending to pressures that imply you are "nothing without a man"? Are you wrong to relish the good parts if there are bad or inadequate parts?

Although most of us realize (and the rest of us should!) that no relationship will ever be perfect, we are constantly bombarded with the idea of everlasting bliss, as this woman describes:

"I was raised with the idea that my permanent relationship would be one where romance flourished every single second of the day. I would be permanently attracted to my mate, and nothing would ever get us down, we would live on love, and I would feel like a queen every day of my life after I married him. Oh, and we would never fight—if we did, it meant that it was a 'bad' relationship."

Are Women "Masochists" If They Stay in Imperfect Relationships? (Is It Anti-Feminist for the New Woman to Live with a Chauvinist?)

There is great pressure on women to be "successful" in their personal lives—which means to be "happy," "stable," and eventually get married, and they are often put down if they are in a relationship that is not "happy":

"I love my boyfriend very much, but we fight a lot. Too much; I am trying to change this. I get so sick, though, of people asking me why I stay and don't give him up. 'I love him,' I say! They think if it's not perfect, I should leave. I'm tired of this."

Usually, unhappy relationships do not start out badly; often they begin with intense attraction and emotional involvement, so that later, when the man doesn't show the basic sharing and caring skills a woman had enjoyed so much, she may still stay, hoping that this new behavior is a temporary problem—and that the initial loving behavior, the "good part" will return.

But if a woman talks too much about the problems in her relationship, some of her friends may start saying, "Why do you stay? Aren't you being masochistic?" Or, if a woman who is having a particularly unhappy day should tell someone, "My personal life is in turmoil," she is likely to be met with this attitude, spoken or unspoken: Can't she get it together? What's the matter with her?

Calling women "masochists" is another example of the ways in which women have been made into scapegoats and blamed for almost everything that goes wrong. We are challenging this mislabeling here. What really happens in relationships that become unhappy is that they *change:* in the beginning the involvement usually *is* happy, but as the stereotypes we saw in chapter 1 gradually creep in and the woman tries to fight against them, the situation starts to deteriorate. Even when faced with problems, most women try to stay and make it work—but all too often their reward for this loyalty is to be labeled a "masochist." Surely, if women left at the first sign of trouble, they would be called selfish, disloyal and callous?! Are women in a no-win situation?

"I don't understand why the society we live in (TV, music, politics, work) still has this underlying thing that says: women are needy and weak because that's the way they are. It's so obvious we've been labeled that way because of a natural response to being looked down on. I mean, isn't that clear?"

"I always said this was a great country, and I still think so. But I can't quite believe how much subtle bullshit I have to put up with just because I'm a woman, now that I'm out in the 'real world.' I guess in my college ivory tower I didn't have to deal with it. But it seems to me to be one of the most undemocratic situations I can imagine for such a 'great,' 'democratic' nation. This is all played out in miniature in relationships, too."

The point is that in many problematic relationships, there are also some good parts: sometimes a woman loves a man who is not able (or doesn't want) to sustain a lasting day-to-day working relationship, but the relationship and her feelings toward him are still deeply moving and important to her. After all, love is not just a knee-jerk response to someone who is "nice" to us!

"My friends and my mother hate this man, but I love him, I really do. He does not commit to me in a total sense, I don't have rights to his time or privacy, and, yes, I wish I did. But the fact remains that I don't . . . that is who he is. And I choose to see him . . . just because it's not a textbook relationship doesn't mean I should judge it so harshly, or that anyone else should."

Is "happiness" always the goal in a relationship?

As this woman explains, the "good stuff" for her is the feeling she has for her partner, not something she gets out of the relationship:

"He's the one I want to love. Some other man might be easier, more talkative, but I don't love them. I love him for the person that he is, I love a *person,* not a relationship. I'm not looking for a person to give me the best relationship there is, I'm looking for a person I feel connected to."

A relationship can be very unstable, or even unhappy, and still provide a kind of nourishment for the soul. Sometimes, an unstable relationship opens doors in you that a comfortable, smooth relationship does not. It is your choice.

Sometimes women say that even the love they feel in a

rough relationship gives them more pleasure, more of a feeling of being themselves and being alive than they might find in a more "stable" or "pleasant" relationship:

"I don't look at my relationship as a source of happiness. I am the source of my own happiness. I look to it for giving me what it gives me, not giving me a particular thing that I'm supposed to *require.* I love him because of who he is, what he is, what we are together. Sometimes it is 'happy,' sometimes it is not. I choose to stay because I feel a deep sense of trust with him, and feel fulfilled at least 75 percent of the time. That is enough for me."

If it has no future, is it a waste of time?

Some women say that they are having love affairs which, even though they are obviously not going to last, are very meaningful to them. A love affair that is not stable is not necessarily a failure if it gives you something you need—as long as it is not emotionally or physically violent.

There is no shame in finding ourselves in imperfect, flawed relationships. If we give all of ourselves, our love, our allegiance, and then are "betrayed," or if the person we love changes, this does not mean we should not have given ourselves in the first place. We have not made a mistake because we loved. The beauty of loving, of having loved, is part of "the good stuff."

How happy is a "normal" relationship?

Exactly how much of what you want from a relationship should you be getting? How "good" does "good" have to be? How imperfect is awful? And when does imperfect become insufferable?

"It was years before I could appreciate my own relationship without all the tapes playing in my head about us not being married, me making more money than he did, we didn't have children, and on and on. I thought I wasn't really 'grown up,' this relationship didn't measure up somehow. But good grief! It makes me happy! Why do I have to live somebody else's idea of my life?"

If you are getting 70 percent of what you want, is this OK? Is 80 percent OK? To the outside world? To you?

Perhaps you would rather be on your own if you cannot have 100 percent of the good stuff. Or if you cannot have a relationship in which you never hear condescending remarks, never have to witness him acting as though he is superior to you, and in which you don't have to waste energy trying to get him to talk, really talk and listen. You could be making the right choice. It all depends on *your* life and *your* needs. There is no measuring stick that you have to use to assess the value of your relationship, although our culture would love you to.

Not Having Anywhere to Talk About the Bad Stuff

Most women say that, although they usually can talk deeply to one or two best friends, it's really hard to tell them the complete truth about the frightening emotional times in their relationship:

"I didn't tell my sister what happened because I knew she would say, 'Why don't you leave if he did that?' And she wouldn't remember all the good things he does."

We can be in very "good" relationships, ("good," in this sense, meaning satisfying, fulfilling), but still find that somehow we have to hide the bad times, especially the worst times, from friends and family. Often, we feel they will chastise and look down on us for staying:

"He is very passionate, and when we argue he raises his voice and stomps around the apartment. I sort of like this quality, his 'Italian Papa' trait. It's the same part that is so passionate in bed. But my two friends who live downstairs have decided that I am in a shitty relationship, and they look shocked when they see us cuddling and cooing an hour later. Why can't they see that the fights are the best way we have, so far, of working through things? And what has it got to do with them, anyway? Why do they have to be so judgmental? So 'superior'?"

"Our fights are wearing me down. We do it almost every night, and in the morning I go to work feeling lousy. I talked to my girlfriends about the problems when I first got involved with him, but now I'm too embarrassed: they would just wonder why I stay."

"We only saw his friends, and when I would try to talk to them about the fighting, they would sort of defend him and say, 'You can't keep nagging him or he will leave,' or, 'Don't take it so seriously,'—as if I deserved the treatment! It made me feel even worse, so I stopped talking about it."

Why is it that all too often we can't tell anybody about the really bad things that happen in our relationships? That we feel we will lose our friends' respect if they know just how terrible or humiliating something is?

"Why can't others accept that just because you had a bad time yesterday, it doesn't mean your overall relationship is bad? There is no shame in having problems."

Is it embarrassing because, a man mistreating a woman is like a social slur, a symbol of women's "powerlessness" and inequality?

The first point to make is that compromising over *some* things in *some* ways doesn't mean you don't know your own mind. Accepting some bad parts of a relationship may be your way of getting some good things or a temporary way of exploring certain feelings you have, aspects of another person that you want to know more about. Again, no relationship or person is flawless, and it is not antifeminist to accept flaws. Remember, feminism is about *choice.*

The second point is to realize that our society has a damaging and overly black-and-white standard for women in relationships. If women are constantly being told that they are "masochists" to stay in a not-so-perfect relationship, it stands to reason that they are going to stop talking to their friends about their problems. This fear of being labeled a "masochist," plus feelings of loyalty to a person one loves, make women keep quiet just at the time they need their friends most.

This is the tragedy of the situation: if you can't really talk to your friends about what is going on, it makes it harder to think through your problems and resolve them —harder to separate the "bad" from the "good," enjoy the good and accept (or change) the bad, or decide to leave.

Enforced Isolation

One woman tells how the spiral of not talking to friends leads to isolation:

"I didn't tell anyone for ages that I felt angry and resentful a lot of the time. I kept it bottled up inside because I wanted people to think we had a good relationship, that I had it all together, was on top of it all. I was always thought of that way. I'm a lawyer, and no one else from my neighborhood even went to college. So I had these two lives: one with this sophisticated guy that was complex and difficult, and with whom I had a turbulent relationship, and the other with this group of down-to-earth, family-oriented people who could consider him a rich, arrogant, abusive snob. And they would consider me stupid for hanging around with him. I felt very isolated and alone."

When you can't tell your friends what is really bad in your relationship (it may be a small percentage of what goes on, but nevertheless awful), you lose contact with them. You have to lie to them and can't really be honest and comfortable. As this is not likely to help you deal with your relationship either, the whole situation can gradually deteriorate.

Often, women find that they are loneliest even when they are in a bad relationship—much lonelier than when they are "single." They can't talk to their partner, and they can't talk to their friends. One woman has her own way of avoiding alienation from her friends:

"I have these friends from college (we'll all be forty this year). Once a month or so, we get together and really rag on our husbands and boyfriends. It works like a charm. And it's safe: it's just us, nothing we ever say gets repeated. And no one expects anyone to say the same thing next time or 'explain' everything. I can't describe it. It's heaven."

Usually, if you tell a friend, "Last night he . . ." and then the next day you enthuse over how much you are looking forward to seeing him, the friend will look at you with some desire for an explanation or embarrassment, unless you explain how you resolved the situation last night. We should start realizing that a friend should feel free to discuss problems with us, and this does not mean that we should judge her or question the reasons she has for staying with someone who "did something like that." We should be able to discuss the problems in each other's relationships without being told we are being "disloyal" to our partners and without the implied question: If you don't like it, why don't you leave him? How else can we understand the problems and try to work out the solutions?

Finally, remember: while you're feeling worried and guilty about a compromise you have just made in your relationship, your friends may be feeling similarly worried that *you* wouldn't approve of some of the things going on in *their* relationships! They may be feeling guilty too. If we could only talk to each other without the fear that we're unacceptable, we would feel less isolated, more sure of ourselves, and give each other more emotional support— plus, have fun talking about things. The dynamic of labeling women "masochists" is a part of the damaging emotional contract we need to change; many women are also subscribing to it. Silence among women, because of fear and intimidation, is another mechanism by which society alienates women from each other, dividing (and conquering) them.

If You Satisfy Your Own *Needs, Do You Feel Selfish?*

Do you have a vague, nagging feeling that you should be doing more for him, that you should love him more, find more things to do to make him happy? Quite a few women say they somehow feel guilty if they simply take the relationship and enjoy it on their own terms. They feel they are "using" it:

"He makes dinner for me almost every night. I come home from work, (his office is at our home) and he's already there, making it. He has done all the shopping— everything. This is really nice, although there are a lot of other things wrong with the relationship. I can't tell if he really likes doing this, or if it's his way of trying to make up for some of the bad parts—which he won't talk about directly. I didn't know whether to relax and enjoy it, or whether I should be getting out of the relationship—or if one day he's going to turn to me and tell me how unfair I am, how I'm exploiting him through his doing all the cooking! What a nineties problem!"

"At home or at his place, I go around in sloppy old clothes, sometimes in curlers. I work and don't talk much, I'm not very sociable. Then when we go out with our friends, I turn on the charm. I wear all my makeup and

everything. I like going around the house with no per-
fume, no makeup, but I worry I'm not keeping up my end.
Shouldn't I make more of an effort to look civilized? Try
harder to be sexy?"

Another woman worries that she likes her relationship
for the "wrong" reason: that it's not what relationships are
supposed to be about, not emotionally developed:

"I am a playwright, and the biggest thrill is when he
walks in with me before a performance. All dressed up, I
feel really elegant. He wears his navy suit and looks so
impressive, plus it's good to know he is beside me, rooting
for me. But we don't have something deep, he's not someone I fell head over heels in love with, he probably doesn't
understand what I think my plays are really about. Yet he's
perfect for me in many ways. He takes me home after the
show, or we go out to eat. It's a great luxury. What I worry
about is that maybe's it's not fair to him that I'm using him
like this. He enjoys everything too, but, I don't know,
shouldn't I have great passion? Do I like him too much for
his appearance? Men have been that way so long with
women, I feel guilty for doing the same to *him*."

Or sometimes women feel guilty for enjoying things
they're not "supposed" to enjoy:

"I feel that in some deep way he will take care of me.
This is probably very unliberated and very bad—I know I
should be more self-sufficient—but I like him to take care
of me. I like it when he pays for my dinner in a restaurant.
It's terrible, I know."

"The other day we had a picnic. We went up into the
hills, and he grabbed me and fucked me right there! I

loved it! I loved feeling totally in his power. What my friends would say, I hate to think!"

"A grown-up woman isn't supposed to like being chucked under the chin, or called 'baby.' But I feel so feminine and adored when he does these things. Am I retarded?"

Are you taking advantage of him if you go around in curlers; if you are not sexy every evening; if you enjoy his macho moments in bed? Of course not, as long as no one is being hurt.

What is a "Good" Relationship?

As we have already stated, there are many kinds of good relationships, not just one standard model that everybody must match up to. And the kind you want at one period in your life may not be the kind you want later. The important thing to remember is to make the right choice, whatever it is, for you today, and to be true to yourself when you make it.

Here are several types of relationships: which appeals to you for your life now?

"We decided to live together about a year ago. Our relationship is that we care deeply about each other and show it in small ways, like daily companionship, saving money to buy something for our home, giving each other a backrub when we are really tired, cooking for each other

—the basic pleasures! I like the security of knowing he is there for me."

"My boyfriend is a pilot. We see each other for a long weekend once a month. I was married once before—the 'standard type'—and I didn't like it. I need some space. I sure have it now! Now, I can be independent, yet fulfilled emotionally. My life has balance."

"We go out about once a week. It's great. We go to parties, usually, where we have lots of friends. We belong to a dancing society, so usually there is a lot of wild dancing and music—Latin, jazz, MTV. It's a ball to get dressed up and *go*. I look forward to it all week."

"Really loving is an earthy thing. It's putting up with dirty clothes on the floor, cleaning up the bathroom after he's been sick in there, coming back when you're really mad at him, sitting by his side night after night as he watches TV programs you hate. This love we have is gentle and quiet and unassuming. It's constant and supportive. It's forgiving."

"We married in '87 and have a beautiful eighteen-month-old daughter. The things I like to do are not career-oriented, and I feel blessed to be able to do what I want and not be tied down to a paying job. Maybe it sounds 'unliberated' or too traditional to spend my time caring for my daughter, making our house beautiful, giving dinner parties for friends (I love to cook!). But I really don't think it is—I do these things because I *choose* to. A lot of the time, I notice other women have this expression of disdain, like, 'You don't *work?* You "just" stay *home?*' What I say to that is, what, are you kidding? This is *GREAT!* It's a luxury."

Which of these relationships would you choose? Maybe you have even another notion of your ideal. Maybe you've decided that you don't want a relationship at all. What matters is what *you* want. It is *your* choice.

"How good" is your relationship?

Here are some questions to ask yourself about your relationship to help you to see if it is "good" and "happy" in your terms:

- Are you "in love" now? How can you tell?
- Do you like being in this relationship? Is it one of learning, enlightenment? Are there painful ups and downs, but are they fulfilling? Is there joy? Ambivalence? How important is it?
- What is the most important part of your relationship? Is it love, passion, sex, money, daily companionship, or the permanence of a long-term involvement? What is the *real* reason you want it?
- Are you "happy" with the relationship? Inspired? Can you imagine spending the rest of your life in it? What would you like to change?
- Is the love you are giving and receiving the kind you want? Have you seen another type in a friend's relationship, in a book or a film that you would find more thrilling?

- Do you feel guilty enjoying a relationship that is not seen by your family, friends, and people in general as "right" or "happy," although you think it is worthwhile?
- Do you want permanence in the relationship —whether or not you have it? Do you feel guilty about wanting/not wanting permanence?
- Do you feel guilty about liking parts of the relationship that you know might be considered "unliberated"? What are they? Him talking baby talk to you? Having unusual sexual fantasies? Getting dressed up and acting "feminine"? Letting him take care of the finances?
- Who is making the most money? Paying the most for things? How do you feel about it?

How to Celebrate Your Relationship! (and Revel in the Good Stuff)

If you have answered all these questions and you are sure that what you have is on the high side of the worth-having scale, why wait? Enjoy. We give you total permission! In fact, we insist!

Here's how some women told us they do just that:

"On Fridays after work we go buy our favorite snacks, rush home, put our pyjamas on (yes, I mean it!), grab the cats, the dog, my son (Ethan, three), and we watch cartoons and old movies in bed. We stay there all evening. My son makes up stories and tells them to us. We wallow in our closeness and in what we have together, and I look over at this man and I think, 'If I spent every Friday night like this for the rest of my life, it wouldn't be too many.' "

"My favorite time is when we lie in bed together and talk, late at night. We tell each other anything that's on our minds—silly jokes, deep ideas, things we're upset about. Or we listen to music. We make love about three times a week, sometimes it's just playing around (sometimes one of us jerks off while the other utters encouraging words), then drifting off to sleep. Great."

"I found a book of love poetry which is an anthology of all the greats. Neither of us are literary at all, but we read these to each other and it's our special treat. Last night he read me parts of *The Prophet* by Kahlil Gibran, which is so pretty, and then I read him a sonnet by William Shakespeare. We took candles into our bedroom (just a bed and walls, no more room!). It was so peaceful. We made love very slow, and I had that feeling of belonging, of being home. This doesn't happen that often, if it did it wouldn't be a celebration."

"He talks very tenderly to me at first. *Then*—we peel off each other's clothes and rub our bodies together. I feel so aroused when we do this. Then he'll start telling me some really sexy erotic fantasy he has about me and what we are doing, as he puts his finger just at the opening of my vagina, or on my clitoris, to tease me, make me hunger for more. I get really excited, and sometimes I masturbate myself during all this. Then, when I can't stand it anymore, I climb on top of him and he bangs into me—which I love— until he comes in one shuddering massive convulsion. Then he falls back, telling me how he loves me.''

"We have a lot of shared interests, and our most fun days are when we do them together: go out for the afternoon, snoop around antique shops, find little things we want to buy, eat ice cream (that we shouldn't), go to a movie later. Then go home and have dinner, or visit friends. It's the best feeling in the world to spend a day with the man you love, and share all those things—then go to sleep later, knowing you have enjoyed it all together. There doesn't even have to be sex.''

"I like that he always tells me I am beautiful and that he loves me. He makes me feel I am the center of his universe. I like that he desires me and always gets turned on around me. I like his body and the way he is, his personality and his soul, the expressions on his face and the gestures of his hands. When he takes me in his arms, well, I forget everything but his smell, his sounds, the warmth of our bodies.''

"I was not interested in a commitment. I was just trying to have fun. But I had dinner with Mr. Adorable and I've never looked back. Sure, there are things that aren't ideal about him. There are things about me that aren't ideal. That doesn't mean you can't give each other the stars!

"We're married and live in the city with our new puppy. We love each other more than we ever have. Sometimes I feel so full, I can't believe it. Sunshine in my stomach.''

Men love to revel too!:

"The most in love and romantic day of my life was in graduate school. I was seeing this girl (sorry, woman, but she was twenty) and she was at school up near Boston. We planned a tryst in Connecticut. There was a blizzard, so of course I thought all our plans would be blown, but it was OK. I took the train up and she took one down. I pulled into the station and through the snowfall I could see her, all alone, in a long wool skirt and boots and coat and hat; I jumped off before we'd even come to a stop! We went to this inn that I had heard about and I blew all my money on a roast beef dinner in front of the fire and many brandies after that. We went outside after dinner and the town was so perfect, so white and so quiet. We made love all night long. I felt I had been looking for her forever."

"She is the greatest, so beautiful and I love her so much. Dignity, warmth, sexiness, humor. Today when I walked to work I felt like the luckiest fellow in town. I think of her in her red dress at her office and I can't wait to get home, where we will make love, shower, eat out somewhere, talk, sleep. I hope to God this never leaves us."

"We like to just hang around our house. We're not party types. We like sweatpants and pizza and W.C. Fields movies, but all night we *cuddle!*"

"I like intercourse more psychologically than physically. If the physical sensation was all I wanted, masturbation would be enough. There is a joining of spirits and souls when intercourse is good that is hard to describe, but it is marvelous. Good intercourse usually means things are going well in the relationship, we are happy with each other."

With all the magazines out there warning you that you are probably neurotic for being in a "less than perfect" relationship, we hope you will now have a more realistic view of the whole picture. It is important to know that even if your relationship isn't perfect, there is no need to feel guilty for taking great pleasure in the things you *do* get out of it. Certainly there are gradations and not every relationship is worth staying in. But don't feel guilty if you think yours is. Remember, it is your opinion that counts.

It is a wonderful thing to find a relationship that works for you. It is apparent that this is not something that happens every day. If you are in a relationship that is fulfilling you, good for you! Enjoy!

6

How to Be Single and Love It (When All Around Are Panicking)

"Being single is the greatest. I can do anything I want, I'm free! I have more energy because I'm not caught up in learning about and negotiating with another person full-time. All that adjusting. I putter around the house, read books, go to movies, eat in restaurants, dance, travel, see my friends. I would say I have *fun.*"

"I love my life! How funny, I never said that when I was in my last relationship—I always said, 'I love *him.*' But now I can honestly say that my life has never before been so fulfilling. People wonder why I am not attached, why some 'lucky guy' hasn't 'grabbed' me. That makes me want to laugh. What an antiquated way of thinking. *I* feel like the lucky person; I have *myself!*"

Women Love Being Single

Most single women say that, no matter what the problems, they love their freedom and independence, the fun of meeting and knowing different people and being able to call their lives their own:

"I love doing what I want—whatever that means. Like lying around, looking like hell, and reading a trashy novel or dressing up in my sexiest garb and dancing my head off at a club."

"Traveling on my own is one of my favorite things. I love the feeling of not being tied down by another person, being the only one responsible for myself. Not reporting to anyone. If I meet someone I want to share all this with, OK. But right now this is the way I like it."

"It's great to design your own life. To flirt with anyone you want, bring them home if you want—or not if you don't! To have your home just the way you want it, with no one to argue with about housework, no one else's taste to consider."

Many women, particularly those who were in unsatisfying long-term relationships before, revel in their freedom:

"No matter how bad a day is now, it's 100 percent better than when I was in my relationship."

"If I want to cook dinner at seven or nine, or not at all, then I can. If I don't do the laundry for two weeks, I am the only one to complain, if I want to read in bed half the night, I can. And if on Saturday I look like a witch, and don't get dressed all day, it's my choice. I like being responsible for myself and knowing that I can make it on my own, that I am the only one I have to depend on. The disadvantages are not having that someone special who understands me and loves me, not being able to give all the love I have. But my sex life is great. I have three or four men whom I see occasionally and I thoroughly enjoy it."

"I'm open for love to happen but it's just not that important to me right now. My own self, work and friends are numero uno. I love being single. I'm celibate. I don't seem to find it necessary to be involved. Independence! I'm free! I love going alone to parties, restaurants, shopping, movies. Sometimes I feel like going with others, so I go with friends, but sometimes I just 'want to be alone,' and since this is something I didn't have in my marriage, I'm still relishing it. Sometimes others try to make me feel as if there is something terribly wrong with me for being alone, but that's their problem."

Most Women are Single Half Their Lives!

What about the idea that all "grown-up women" are either married "with" someone? Aren't real women "married with children"?

If you count the number of years (after age eighteen) before a woman is married, then add in the years after a possible divorce or between marriages (a 50 percent divorce rate is standard in urban areas), and the number of years a woman may be a widow (since women usually live much longer than men), you will find that the average woman is single for *half* of her adult life. In other words being single is "normal"!

"What's a nice girl like you doing without a man?"

"Sometimes I think even if I were a new Mozart, it wouldn't be enough. All my friends and family would still be saying, 'And when are you getting married? Are you seeing anybody?' "

Although most women say they like being single, many do feel the pressure "out there" to *not* be single, to be "looking for a man."

"I get so sick of people saying that they wish I would find some nice young man and settle down. I don't want to, it's as simple as that. I wonder if they are ever going to stop saying this!"

"It's as if everyone thinks of you as a reject, defective— as though they think, 'If someone hasn't married her yet, there must be something wrong with her!' "

"I just hope that someday my family and friends will believe I mean it when I say I am happy without a committed relationship. I know it's hard for them, they want to see me happy, but why can't they believe that I *am?* I resent their insinuation that I am a poor little wretch who has to put up her Christmas lights alone and has no one to share her TV dinners with. I hardly have any time alone as it is! I'm always with people. If they don't stop hassling me, I won't keep up my relationships with them."

Why all the prejudice against single women? Isn't it OK to be alone, to like it? Do you *have* to be in a relationship or to be looking for one to be "normal"? If you decide that you dislike relationships, why does the world think you are "weird"?

Eighties media images of single women

Single women in the eighties were depicted as unstable, both sexually and emotionally—the film *Fatal Attraction* was a good example. Also, single women were often portrayed on television as angry, embittered, often untrustworthy, neurotic, and "needy." Study after study has shown that this is not true, it is single women who are happier, married women who feel more dissatisfied. So why all of this negativity?

Of course, in the seventies the media stereotyped women differently: then, married women were supposed to be the "dull," "stupid" ones while single women were supposed to be "free" and "hip." Now, with AIDS and the conservative mood in many Western countries, the images have been reversed: single women are seen as not fulfilling their "natural" role, and we are endlessly bombarded with magazine articles about women who "gave up" their careers—in fact, couldn't *wait* to give them up—for the fun and glorious experience of having babies (it is supposedly impossible to have both). This has happened at least once before: after World War II there was a massive media campaign to get women to return to the home and let men have the jobs. However, statistically, the number of women working outside the home has increased steadily throughout the twentieth century, and today the great majority of women, married *and* single, are employed.

The stereotyping of single women by the media in the eighties reached a crescendo with a 1986 cover of *Newsweek:* "The Marriage Crunch—If You're a Single Woman, Here Are Your Chances of Getting Married, with a drawing of a miserable woman staring at the wall of her lonely apartment." The article was prompted by a study conducted by two Yale sociologists and a Harvard economist (their methodology was later proved incorrect), who claimed that thirty-year-old women who were still single had only a 20 percent chance of getting married and that forty year olds who were still single were more likely to be killed by a terrorist than find a husband! Fighting words— and words that assumed we are all on a hunt for a husband, and miserable if we fail.

Whatever you may feel about marriage, one thing is certain: with or without media "nagging" (a great new use for that word!), women are making their *own* choices, and those choices include being single for more and more of our adult lives.

What are Single Women's Lives Really Like?

According to most women, being single is nothing like media stereotypes. While women may love men, they also love the way they can live on their own. They love to run their own lives, have the luxury of paying full attention to their jobs, have time for their friends, children, and not least, for themselves. They enjoy being able to think freely without having to explain anything, being able to create their own lives.

As one woman puts it, "There is joy in commitment to a relationship that works; but there is also great joy in a committed relationship with *yourself*."

Two women describe their typical day:

"I feel so happy, I want to shout it from the rooftops, 'I'm free, I'm free.' Free to run my life the way I want, do what I want. You may think I'm in that initial elation that comes when you break out of a stifling, painful love, and you may be right—but what a glorious feeling to have unlimited days, freedom, autonomy. It's been six months, and I still feel like I've been let out of prison. I don't think there's anything wrong with love, in fact I think it's beautiful. But I never knew how beautiful it was to call your life your own. I've had a boyfriend since I was fifteen, different ones, but they were one right after the other—like I learned was the thing to do for a girl to be successful. I had no idea being 'alone' could be so much fun. I wish women were taught that a little bit more.

"One thing that really bugs me is seeing pity in people's eyes when I tell them I live alone, with Belinda (my Maine coon cat) and do things on my own. They obviously think this is really sad, that I probably have some hang-ups, or 'problems' that keep men at a distance or scare them away or 'turn them off.' 'You're so pretty, you ought to have a beau,' they say, and so on. They must fantasize that I spend horrible, desolate evenings crying in bed and scanning the personals or going out on unsuccessful blind dates.

"The silliest part of people feeling sorry for me because I'm alone so much is that I hardly spend any time alone! I spend more time with people than I did when I was in a relationship. My life is far from lonely—in fact, it seems saturated with people.

"My typical day is so full, I can hardly keep it straight; but it goes something like this:

7:00 Get up, feed Belinda, turn on the news, shower, meditate, dress, call my mom or a friend.
8:30 Either a breakfast meeting or go to my favorite café and talk to my friend Phyllis who has a fabulous job with

a philanthropist and tells me great stories of their travels.

9:00 Get to office at nine sharp. I love my work—I'm in advertising, and although this may sound snotty, I'm very good at it. Sometimes it's exhausting and overwhelming, when I'm really swamped, but I love it. I'm right where I want to be work-wise. I get paid very well, too.

12:00 Lunch, either business or errands with a friend, or go to the park with a friend from work (I have three that I really care for). We go to the park and rehash the previous evening and crack each other up.

5:30 Hopefully get out of the office in time to hit the gym, where I have a trainer three times a week who works me like a mule. I work out, take a steam bath where I usually see my friend Pam, shower, go home.

7:00 By now I'm home in my little apartment which I love. It has all *my* things in it, my taste. I don't think I could ever bear to share it with someone! When I get in from the gym, I return calls, open mail, feed Belinda, and play with her. If I'm going out, which I do four to five nights a week, I get dressed and prepare to go on a date, see friends, go dancing, or some other fun thing. This city is great for all that. But sometimes I go to a spiritual workshop I have joined.

11:00 I try to be home by now because I love to cuddle with my cat and talk on the phone, read a good book, watch TV.

12:30 I like to say a prayer, thankful for another day of living.

"Sure, sometimes I have shitty days, just like other people, but they certainly aren't because I'm single!"

"Do I like being single? Well, yes, if I understand your meaning. More important is do I like being Anna, which I do most of the time. 'Singleness' is not something I really think about, it's sort of a modern 'label' isn't it? The thing that men love being single and women hate it? I must have strange friends, because that's the opposite to the way they are. Most of the men we know want to tie us down and we are always trying to avoid being cornered.

"I'm thirty-one and work as a chef in Los Angeles. I make pretty good money, and live near the university. I drive a beat-up Honda and have a German shepherd named Nina. I have lived with two men in my life, one for two years and one for three. I guess you could say the relationships 'failed,' because they didn't last. But they were very important for me at that time, and these men were what I wanted and liked at that time. Now the men I like are very different. I'm seeing one guy on and off (maybe every other Saturday night) who owns a restaurant (not mine) and we hang out and drink wine at his restaurant, while he sees people and talks and table-hops and tells people to go to my restaurant if he is overbooked! We close the place late and go back to my house and have sex and sleep, then in the morning he leaves after breakfast. No commitment, and that's the way I want it, though it took a while to explain that to him. He understands now. I guess I'm a very solitary and private person, and it's really cool to have someone who respects that and understands I don't want to be a 'significant other' or 'girlfriend.'

"I come from a big family in Santa Barbara (not the rich part!) and Nina and I go up there usually every other weekend to see them. I have a goddaughter (my brother's oldest), and I like to spend time with her, my parents, and whoever else is around. I usually get roped into cooking for them one night, because we are Italian and that is my specialty. I always resent this for a second, but then I feel really good to be feeding them and making them happy with something I can do for them.

"Most nights I spend working at the restaurant, so my free time is during the day. I'm heavy into exercise—how Californian, but true! When you're around food as much as me, you have to be. So Nina and I run every morning along the beach, and then go to a coffee shop nearby to have breakfast. I know the people in the coffee shop and the newspaper store, you know, it's very community oriented. I take a class in photography at the university this term (I take a class every term) and it meets four mornings a week, so Nina and I go over there and I drop her with my aunt who lives around the corner.

"My nights off I hang out with my friend M. sometimes, or my friends B. and E. who are married, or I try and see F. who takes me dancing. We have sex sometimes, but not much.

"Do I like my life? Is it full? I love my life, I love all the different components in it. My priorities are hard work, family, time alone, health, and learning. I would like to travel a little more, and I may go to Italy for a year to study. Anything is possible!"

Despite the stereotype of the single woman as basically unfulfilled and "neurotic," most single women's lives are spent working, seeing friends, taking care of family—not pining away in some lonely corner in a rumpled robe, watching soaps and eating chocolate.

"But wouldn't you *rather* be married?"

What does being "alone" really mean? Interestingly, more women say they feel lonely *inside* a nonloving relationship than they do being "single." The main reason for this is that it is much more isolating and terrifying to be with someone you cannot reach than to be on your own, enjoying your life and your friends, "reaching yourself."

Over and over again, women say that they have many great women friends, sometimes friends of a lifetime, and that their communication with them is the closest of all their relationships. So it is not surprising that single women feel less lonely. They have more time to be with their women friends because their time and energy is not consumed in a relationship; they are more likely to feel "heard" and "seen" on a daily basis:

"I think I had a kind of constant, low-grade depression when I was with him. But it wasn't till I was out of the relationship that I realized it. He used to shut me out, close himself off. I *was* alone, even though we were together. In my life now, I have great friendships where I am never shut out. I don't feel lonely at all, now that I am single."

"I'd say one of the greatest gifts of living on my own has been discovering the depth and quality of my friendships. I hadn't had enough time for them before, as I had always been so wrapped up in my marriage. Now I have friendships which fulfill me far more than that relationship ever did, and I can really be there for my friends. It's a whole new way of life I'm discovering."

Social Hassles You Know and Detest

Fighting the stereotypes is no picnic

You know those times when you are expected to be "with someone," "escorted," or "attached"? In these situations, women say that though *they* are perfectly content with being on their own, others project feelings of ner-vousness and condescension onto them—as if they don't really believe the "single woman" is single by choice. What is she doing there, anyway? Somehow her situation is embarrassing, and they think she is probably out to "get her hands" on every guy in the place. As one woman points out, the assumption is not only that women should be married, but also that if they are not, they are probably trying to "trap" men into it:

"I still don't understand why everyone always thinks women are trying to get some guy to marry them. People seem to think that any woman who is not married is dying to get hitched. They never say that about men, at least I've never heard it. And even if she did want to get married, what would be so bad about that? It's as though the most disgusting and undesirable thing in the world for a woman is to want to get married, and the most appealing thing in the world for a man is to avoid it!"

Desperate "predators" out to get their man!

In a social atmosphere, single women are all too often seen as desperate predators who can't be trusted. One woman tells a story about coming face-to-face with the as-sumption that she couldn't possibly be out alone by choice:

"Yes, sure, I can tell you about stereotypes! I was sitting in bed the other afternoon after a luxurious nap, the sun was streaming in the window. I felt so good—I had cleaned my place, been to an art gallery with a friend, and spent the afternoon reading the paper. Now I had an over-whelming urge for Indian food. I *had* to have it . . . there was nothing for it but to take myself to my favorite Indian restaurant.

"When I got there, the guy who is usually at the door greeted me and said, 'I can't understand why such a lovely girl is eating alone this evening.' It doesn't bother me with him, because he is nice and really doesn't understand that this is OK with me. Anyway, it wasn't condescending. But what really annoyed me was this guy who was sitting alone, staring at me. I made it quite clear to him that I didn't want to be stared at and was enjoying my own company. You know, there are definitely ways you can show this while not being rude. Most sensitive people with manners would pick up on it.

"Well, not this fella. First he sent a waiter over with a drink. I told the waiter to thank the gentleman, but I was 'enjoying a dinner alone and don't drink.' When the waiter went over to him to say that, he started laughing! The idiot obviously thought there was no way that I was telling the truth, that I must be playing hard to get, because the only reasons a woman ever goes to a restaurant alone are 1) she can't find anyone to take her, or 2) she wants to get picked up/laid/paid for/meet her future husband.

"I went to the bathroom and when I returned, he was sitting at my table! I asked what he was doing there. He laughed again, and said the classic, 'What are you doing going out alone? Some poor bastard really blew it by leaving *you* in the lurch on a beautiful evening like this!' (all said whilst looking at my chest and legs).

"By this time I was so sick of the whole thing, I just asked him to leave. He got all bent out of shape, saying, 'God, what's the matter? A guy tries to talk to you when you come to a restaurant alone, what do you expect? You shouldn't go out alone in that case! Jesus!'

"It was the same old thing again. I go into situations where I am perfectly happy, in fact I don't even think about the fact that I am alone and that it may be weird to some people, and I meet with the same attitudes. It is never acceptable to most people that you are alone because you *want* to be. That is the last reason they ever think of. I have a great life, but people seem to want to take it away from me. They *want* to think that I'm lonely and depressed."

These kinds of hassles, as another woman describes, often result in women having the feeling that they "shouldn't" go out alone, they "ought" to stay at home or be with a man:

"An old friend was getting married and had invited me to the wedding. It was a special invitation for me, because we had known each other so long and had fallen out at one point.

"It never occurred to me that I would take anyone. I was going to see a lot of friends there, and I didn't want to ask anyone to go with me, I wanted to be free to speak with whoever I wanted and to leave when I wanted to.

"After the ceremony, everyone went to the reception in a beautiful old mansion. I got myself a drink at the bar. I noticed that all the other people at the bar were men—as if women can't get their own drinks. I felt odd, like they thought it was a shame I didn't have someone to wait on me too! When I started to talk to people, every single one asked me who I came with! When I said, 'No one, I came by myself,' one of the women actually frowned and touched my arm and said, in this sort of baby voice, 'Oh, you poor thing! We've got to hook you up with somebody.' It was so uncomfortable. I finally left thinking I was an alien or something. After a while you start to question yourself, too."

Most women have been in situations like these where they are "expected" to be "in a couple" and are looked down upon if they are not:

"Even my women friends are amazed when they meet a woman who is attractive but unattached. If she doesn't have a boyfriend they think she is 1) consumed by her work, 2) emotionally imbalanced, 3) gay, or 4) dysfunctional! Why can't the first idea that pops into their heads be that she is enjoying life by herself?"

Men with commitmentphobia: convincing him you don't want to get married

Many single women say that all the talk in the media about "husband-hungry single women" is having a bad effect on the way men relate to them: many men arrogantly assume that women are "guilty" of this "obsession."

Women are finding it very hard to fight this prejudice which invalidates their every action. No matter what she says or does, the man reacts as if she is "guilty" of "trying to get him," as this woman found:

"Men I know make jokes all the time about the girls they meet, only now the jokes are different. They used to laugh about how women always wanted to stop them from having fun, and about women being clingy. Now they joke about the fact that girls they meet at bars and parties are only looking for a husband. I think all the attention the media and books have given to single women's eternal quest for marriage has hurt us greatly. We already had a hard enough time convincing men that not all of us were trying to trap them into marriage, and therefore couldn't be trusted—we were just "conniving bitches." Now every inch we had gained has been totally blown. We are having to start from scratch."

Another woman describes what happened on a first date she had recently:

"I'm in sales and a man started work here who was very attractive, well dressed, and sexy. He was also very attentive and listened to everything I had to say with what appeared to be interest and sincerity. There seemed to be lots of potential for us to really enjoy each other.

"I was very nervous getting ready for our first date. I hadn't dated in quite a while, no one interested me enough, and I sort of wondered if I had forgotten how to do it! But this guy was different, and I found myself thinking about what it would be like to go to bed with him.

"When he picked me up, he looked adorable. I could feel his excitement too, and he said he had not looked forward to a date this much in a long time.

"We went to a movie (a really good one that put me in a great mood), had a long dinner, talked about our lives. I was enjoying him, and it felt very natural and good.

"When we got back to my place, I asked him up for a nightcap. I fixed us some brandy and put Teddy Pendergrass (my main man) on the stereo. I felt that feeling you get when you're like on the edge of something, you know? During our conversation, he asked me what I was doing over the weekend. I told him I was going to a friend's wedding. I then commented on how many people were getting married, and how weird it was, like they were dropping like flies or something. I asked him if he found the same to be true about his friends, and if he felt odd not being married yet.

"Girl, I saw him blanche! Almost like he had a physical reaction (like to poison). From then on, the conversation deteriorated because he assumed that I was another women out 'to bag him.'

"I was really shocked, you know, because nothing could have been further from the truth. He sat there and went into this long diatribe about how much he resented women he dated who were basically out to get a husband *(him)* and were 'just pretending to be independent.' He said it drove him up a wall to have to listen to women yak on about how much they loved their careers over dinner, when he *knows* that all they really want to do is get hitched and dump the career as soon as possible. He said he felt like 'prey' and was sick of it.

"My first reaction was to tell him I could understand why he would feel like that if some women were only interested in his wallet, where his family lived, et cetera. I told him a similar experience I had had where the first thing a man asked me was whether I liked children, et cetera. I was trying to empathize.

"But he didn't even listen to my side of things. Finally, I explicitly told him that I wasn't interested in marriage at all, and I meant it. I even said the words 'I don't want to get married.' How much clearer can you be? And I felt kind of demeaned, you know, saying that . . . but I thought he should hear it. Well, he withdrew immediately from the moment the whole subject came up, and saw me as some kind of desperate, wimpy enemy. I was so disappointed. We muttered 'good night' and he left."

Here is another woman's reaction to the ridiculous prejudices against single women:

"I walk by bookstores and see all these books on 'how to find a husband in thirty days' and 'getting him to the altar' and I get really pissed off. If *I* see those books, then men must see those books, too. Not to mention all the television shows with audience participation that go on and on about this. Now, when I meet men, they are all wearing this invisible sign which reads, 'Don't even *think* of mentioning marriage in my vicinity.' It is so arrogant. It makes me want to say, the minute I meet one of them, 'Hi, I'm Julie, and I don't want to get married!' "

This is yet another example of the social pressures that contrive to put women on the defensive. And women often remark that all this pressure becomes stronger around the age of thirty.

Thirty and not married: the *terror*?

Interestingly, just at the time when many women begin to consider whether they would like to try marriage and a family because they've reached an age when biologically they should make a decision, they are faced with additional pressure. They can't relax and decide: they are under the gun to decide. How many of us have been asked, "So when are you going to settle down and have children?" as soon as someone—even a comparative stranger—discovers that we're thirty?

We then start to worry about the stereotypes being hurled at us:

"All of a sudden I woke up and realized most of my friends are married and then, Christ, damn, is there something wrong with me, am I going to be single forever? I'm starting to think I'm going to be, starting to cope with that. You wonder what's going to happen when you're older and that kind of stuff. It's a little scary, but I don't really think I'm ever going to get married. And that's dumb because that's like saying, well, can't you take care of yourself?"

"The pressure to get married or find a life partner is great now, mostly internal. I feel that if I don't become involved soon there is something wrong with me. But I don't want to make a big deal about it, or I'll feel like a 'typical' picture of a desperate female trying to drag some poor unsuspecting male up the aisle."

Many single women say they are so assaulted by the assumption that they are desperate to get married that it becomes a real task to maintain their own independent perspective, and not let all this pressure interfere with their enjoyment of living on their own.

It can be very difficult to think clearly about whether we want to be married or to live life on our own, surrounded by such strong social pressure.

One way to defend yourself against this barrage of irrational pressures is to listen to the women, here and all around us, talking about what their lives are *really* like.

The Debate over Whether to Marry

The majority of single women have mixed feelings about marriage, questioning their own feelings and motivations:

"The idea of marriage sounds great—so much love—but what if I hate it? What if my feelings don't last? I've never met anyone I thought I could marry, but I've been proposed to. I don't know, it seems like it would be wonderful to be married, be *sure* of things.''

"I'm in a state of confusion now. I've been involved with different men often enough to realize that I could never have been happy married to any of them. But I feel the need to have a permanent man. Do I *really* need it or is it just something we have been reared to believe—that we need to have a man to make our lives complete?''

Some women say they are just not interested in marriage —they never want to get married, at least not in the foreseeable future:

"Marriage seems overrated—people reaching for a type of security that just doesn't exist anymore. It is based on assumptions that aren't realistic. As a contract, it's very unfair and inequitable. I hope I never get married.''

"The idea of marriage scares me right now. I think it is important for some individuals, but not all. I do not think I am monogamous by nature!''

Even when they are in relationships that they like, some women still do not want to get married:

"We are compatible on all levels—we laugh, we cry, we share many things, the same activities, and we are politically alike—conservative. I can tell my love anything, and usually do! I am extremely happy, and so is he. But as to the future—we are too young to be looking for a lifetime commitment.''

Sometimes these women feel guilty for not wanting the permanence of marriage:

"I love my boyfriend, but I don't want to plan my life with him. I've been seeing him for about a year, and I get sick of all the questions about when we are going to move in together, etc. Why can't I just like it the way it is? Am I shallow? 'Afraid of intimacy'?"

Women who have been married before are often particularly reluctant to remarry:

"As I sit here writing this I feel like I could go on for ages, write a novel, about the bliss of being on my own. It sounds overly dramatic to say that I experience my new single status as if I had been let out of prison, but it isn't, I really feel that way. I feel like I spent eight years denying who I was, living with daily disappointments, denied anger, put-downs and judgments—like I was living in a country where those were the rules. Now I live in another country, one filled with my own choices, my own feelings, one where who I am is celebrated—by me, and my friends. I never again want to live the way I did when I was 'attached.' I couldn't have felt less attached!"

"I had been married for most of my adult life, and am now forty-eight and divorced. I run my own life and do not answer to anyone but myself—I love that. But I don't love being considered 'incomplete,' 'unloved' by so many people. I am fine! Why can't I be seen as what I really am (living on my own and satisfied with that) instead of people trying to insist I must be unhappy, lonely, and a 'loser'?"

But other women, especially some who have never been married, do want the commitment of marriage:

"Intellectually, I realize that people can be single all their lives. I have some role models (women) who are single, and so I feel that I would have some support for a decision to be single. However, emotionally, I seem conditioned towards marriage. Some part of me does not want to be single forever."

A lot of women say they feel embarrassed to "admit" they want marriage (no wonder, with women chided for being "desperate"):

"It's hard to admit I really want a man, I really want a marriage. No matter what I know politically, no matter how impossible or stupid it seems . . . I still want it. But I feel a great deal of pressure not to be preoccupied with love or romantic feelings. Not to get 'carried away' with love."

Some women decide they would like to try marriage after experiencing a series of unsatisfying relationships:

"I want to marry because I don't want to split my love up. I have been in love in the past, and later we fell out of love, and then I went through that whole cycle again, and I don't want to anymore. I want to marry a man I fall in love with, and give him my love and be faithful to him and only him. This would be very satisfying to me."

"It's been fun. All through my twenties I knew a lot of men. Some I loved, some were real pigs. What I really want now is my own gem, and I want him for a long time. I want to have fun at Easter and know at Christmas we can remember Easter. I want to plan a dinner party and know Ed won't have changed to John after I've told all my friends who's coming. And, most of all, I want to really love someone."

But understandably, after what we've heard women say in this book, a lot of single women are wondering if a committed relationship will ever work out for them:

"I don't know, I seem to meet guys who I get involved with but it never lasts—for one reason or another. Usually it's because they want me to be someone I am not, or it is just 'not right' between us. Sometimes I think I had better bring my expectations down a peg or two, or I will be alone forever—never meet anyone. I like my life now, but I would like to have a lasting relationship in my future. But I'm wondering if it will ever happen to me."

"Either I want something lasting and they don't, or they want something lasting and I don't. It never seems to mesh. I'm beginning to think it never will."

The fear that nothing will ever come of their relationships bothers many women; but these women are not "husband hunters"—they simply want to develop deeper relationships.

Should I marry the "wrong guy" or "risk" staying single forever?

What *if* you don't meet "the right man," or someone you really feel good with, someone who is a true addition to your life? With all the pressures we have mentioned, it is not surprising that some women question whether they should "settle" and just marry "someone nice." As one woman says:

"I married to get everyone off my back. He's not fabulous. I was thirty and I just couldn't deal with it anymore."

"I have 'lowered my standards' a lot, because maybe a guy I was not too interested in would be better than no one."

"I keep thinking—if I don't marry this one, I may never marry anyone else. Maybe he's the best I can find."

"All these pressures . . . He's such a nice guy, but, I don't know, there's a lack of enthusiasm I feel, maybe he has a lack of enthusiasm about life, maybe I want too much, maybe I'm a romantic junkie at heart, waiting for Prince Charming or something like that. But why do I have to marry someone I'm not crazy about? On the other hand, I may never find anyone else. Will I be sorry later?"

"As I get older (I'm thirty-seven) I notice the men treat me different (i.e., they don't treat me) than when I was young. It occurs to me I may never find someone good. I feel that I need to be more open to men I might not otherwise look at because I'm sitting here not in a position of power, right?"

"What if I never get married?"

What if I wake up one day and want a baby, and it's too late?

Most women, at some time in their lives, think about whether they want to have a baby. While some women are quite happy to choose to live their lives without children, many fear there is always the possibility, (while their famous "biological clock" is madly ticking away) that they will suddenly wake up one day with a deep, undeniable longing for a child:

"I have always been pretty sure I didn't want a baby, but lately I have been wondering if someday I will want one, and there will be no one to make one with! Plus, I don't know if I could financially manage to have one alone."

"I'm twenty-eight, and have never really thought too much about having a child, except to think how excruciatingly painful it would be physically. But lately I've had these romantic fantasies about being in the delivery room with an adoring husband holding my hand throughout the whole thing. It seems like it would be the most profound experience. I still think I don't want one, but if I'm going to change my mind I should do it before too long."

"I get this tug deep in my belly when I'm around babies. Is that weird? I don't tell anyone about this, though—in my circle, it wouldn't be considered very chic."

"If I live on my own forever, will I be able to afford it?"

Another fear about not marrying concerns money. Many single women, though enjoying their independence, wonder if they will be able to support themselves all their lives. This is not surprising, since many factors make it difficult for women to earn a good wage all their lives, and most women are not taught about life insurance, investments, or general financial strategies. However, the fact is we are doing remarkably well. The highest success rate for new businesses in the United States is held by women who start their own businesses; and it is the women in most families who do the monthly accounting and keep the budget.

Having to carry the financial weight of living on their

own indefinitely is particularly hard for divorced single women with children:

"I love having no one else to answer to financially, but I get worried about money, too. I watch my married friends and how much more they have (materially). I mean, what if I got sick? There would be no money coming in and I would lose my lease and my car very quickly. If I was married, my husband could carry the weight for a while. Or, even if I was in a relationship, at least someone could buy me groceries and stuff. I feel guilty for feeling like this, but it is true."

"I am currently four months pregnant and working for a large corporation. My boyfriend and I plan to get married as soon as we find an apartment. But I'm beginning to wonder if that will ever happen. I sometimes think maybe I'll be bringing up this child alone. I'm frightened. What will happen then? I don't think I can make it."

If you're living on your own now and coping, there is a great chance you will still be able to do this in twenty, thirty, or forty years time. And of course even if you *do* start living with someone, this is no guarantee of permanence or income—for either of you.

The unmentionable fear: getting old

Many younger single women worry, "If I don't get married, won't I wind up alone? Nobody will want me. I'll be old and ugly!" This is the fear that is fed to us day and night: you won't be able to "get a man" especially after forty! The result is that many women think, "I've got to keep trying to meet someone, or maybe just grab the next guy that comes along and settle down before it's too late!"

How many of us wonder about being a "feeble little old lady" at her door, "pathetically" waiting for the milkman, because he is the only person she gets to talk to every day? This is nothing to do with the reality of choosing never to marry, or not to remarry. It is a fantasy encouraged by people who think old is "bad" (and that female "old" is even worse).

Such fears are not based on the *reality* of older women's lives, but they can be very powerful:

"I don't think so much about falling in love right now. I'm too busy! What I am afraid of is growing old alone. Being a dependent old lady. The kind of person everyone has to worry about because she's alone. Pathetic. It's hard to imagine, because my life is so full now. But if I were married, I could have children and grandchildren—I would not end up alone."

"I've always had a fear of having kids—being tied down, always being tired, never having romance or sex again, having less money, blah blah blah. Sort of a man's attitude, really. But a friend of mine asked me the other day: 'but what about when your parents are dead and your man dies —will you want to be alone when you die?' That made me think."

It is quite understandable to be frightened and uncertain about facing the future on your own, however sure you are at the moment that this is what you want. Men feel this way too—it is not only a women's problem. Everyone, at some time or another, has doubts about the choices they make. But listen to these examples of women in their sixties and seventies who are living on their own and loving their freedom. Theirs are inspiring lives and an example to us all!

Older Women—Having a Ball!

The pervasive view that older single women are "unhappy" is not based on older women's own accounts of how they feel:

"The word *single* really irritates me. It sounds so negative! As though I must be miserable and depressed. Pitiable somehow! But I love my life—and everything in it. I've been in relationships before, I was married, but now I choose to be on my own. No one ever seems to view being on your own as a choice. But it is—my life is full and really exciting. I love every minute of it!"

A lot of single women over sixty-five would rate their lives high up on the "happiness scale." Listen to this charming seventy year old:

"I am a seventy-year-old grandma who lives alone, and is very alive. I have two dogs. Love to study and love kids, especially my grandchildren. Right now I'm happy. Tomorrow, who knows?

"My lover died this spring. I miss him. But in a way, I am relieved! I don't miss the put-downs. Since he died, I pass the time reading dime novels. My goals? To write a little, fish, to design. Face death with humor!

"Right now I'm enjoying being single. Usually everyone else—when I'm not single—is more important than I am. Now I'm important and enjoying it! I always looked for love till now. Now all I've got is me, but I don't mind,

I like it. Being single, you can do what you want. Don't have to do anything.

"I admire women who can get up and go. Sally Shelton, Gloria Steinem, Eleanor Roosevelt, Indira Gandhi, Margaret Thatcher, Margaret Mead, Jackie Onassis, Elizabeth Cady Stanton. I believe in the women's movement. I'm a feminist. It made me realize what I'd missed. Although I'm a nurse, I should have been a lawyer.

"I enjoy looking glamorous. Femininity means being sexually pleasing to men, yet firm in one's own ideas. I still shudder at masculine women. I enjoy beautiful clothing— although I live in jeans on a farm. I feed the horses, but can look well when dressed. I don't wear makeup (like Ma). Half the time I look a sight, so I'm not very feminine. Have fun though. If you ask me how I look at seventy, I'd say—truthfully—awful!

"To women today I say: love your kids and encourage them. Then do your own thing. With regard to love, don't worry about happy endings, life doesn't have them! But you can enjoy it meanwhile."

Some older single women certainly dispel myths that they are at home knitting and their sex drive has long since "dried up":

"I am sixty-five years old, have four grown children. I share my love with a seventy-two-year-old man who wants to marry me when I am through with my divorce (my second marriage, thirty-eight years).

Sex with my lover is enjoyable. Usually he stimulates me by hand to orgasm. When we are not together I masturbate. I orgasm easiest through masturbation, but if I do not catch one very soon, I give up and let go without. But most of the time it works."

Some older men also appreciate being older:*

"My enjoyment of sex is as great as it ever was, perhaps more so because my wife has become more knowledgeable with age; she is not shocked or repelled as we may have been when we were first married forty-four years ago. Because we have become more sophisticated, our sex life is different and more enjoyable than it was. There is definitely more variety to it, less embarrassment and reluctance, more acceptance." [age sixty-eight]

"We are in our seventies and been married for five years, and I doubt there is another couple in this country that kisses and hugs each other more times in the average day than we do. We want to be together all we can. This is my wife's third marriage and my second, due to deaths. Sex is always with my wife, I am no woman chaser. I like to lay close to my wife. I love to have my wife lie with her head on my shoulder and her leg laying across my stomach, both satisfied." [over seventy-five]

Thus the stereotype of being "old and alone" is basically inaccurate: most single women over sixty-five like their lives very much. They enjoy their friends, their work, gardens, lovers—all facets of life. While a lack of money can be a definite problem, happiness is a different matter: many women say they feel *happier* when "old and alone"—happier than they ever have been.

---

* From *The Hite Report On Male Sexuality*, Alfred A. Knopf, 1981.

Transition

It can be hard—or at least feel unusual—to start a life on your own after not being single for a while:

"It has been so long since I was 'available' that I sort of don't know what to do. A lot of the rules have changed. Apart from a killer disease out there, I also hear all this talk about the New Man and the 'sensitive guy'—but that's really a crock from what I see. I mean, it just looks like a new way for them to get what they want. They still win in the end, they score big."

"It is stranger than strange to be apartment hunting with my son (he's nine). It's been so long since I've been a part of the singles world that I don't have a clue! And there's this look on people's faces like, You poor thing, which is hard to handle."

"I am panicking and am so glad to be asked about this, it's like confession. I am considering selling the few good pieces of jewelry I have and putting the money away in the bank. I hope I can support myself. I'd better."

But for some women the transition is easy:

"I'm divorced after twenty-eight years of marriage and I love it. I am still OK looking, and right now I have two lovers. Believe it or not, I am a grandmother, too! I have one six-year-old granddaughter and one two-year-old grandson. My kids are a little surprised that I have such an active sex life, but they're getting used to it! Ralph (my main man) cooked the turkey last Thanksgiving, and it was the first time in at least twenty years that I heard laughter at that table. My marriage was based on 'the less said, the better.' Now I have two men who talk and laugh with me, even in bed. I finally have asked for what I like in bed and I am getting it! I have never felt better!"

One woman describes how she has begun to see herself and her relationships with her friends, in a whole new way:

"Being single has been very good for me, but it has been hard, especially at first. I was used to being in a love-less marriage where neither of us was satisfied, but we were financially secure and fitted in with all the social 'shoulds' of being a couple, both working, both successful, etc. I had been with him since grad school, so I had not really lived on my own in the 'real world.' When I decided to leave, after so much agonizing, I found a little apart-ment nearby where some friends lived in the building. They helped me move my furniture, paint the apart-ment . . .

"At first, it was very difficult to adjust to being in my own apartment. I was still grieving over the marriage, the fact that it had broken apart, the sentimentality that hap-pens when you look back and only remember the good times. All my possessions reminded me of 'us' and 'the way it used to be.' I didn't know how to plan my social life so that I would have things to do in the evenings. All my evenings had been spent with him, and all our socializing had been mostly with his friends and business associates. I didn't know how to let it be known that I was a free agent and was ready for a life filled with my own activities.

"The first few months it was summer. It was really hot. I took a leap of faith and rented a share in a house at the beach with several people I didn't know. I went out there every weekend, and it opened up a whole new social life for me. I also invited my own few friends out there, and soon my datebook was crammed.

"I had a fling with a doctor at this time, which was really fun because it reawakened my sexual drive which had been asleep for ages. I was so turned off emotionally with my husband that I had become turned off physically. The doctor was a great lover, and I couldn't get enough! But he got serious very fast, and I wanted my life to be untethered, so I broke it off.

"I am glad I did. My life today is so different from my old life—gone are the endless nights of fighting or silence, of trying and failing to make it work. Drinking and smoking too much because I didn't know what else to do.

"Life can be great, if you choose to do what is best for you. Being single is, so far, my favorite way of living."

The struggle for autonomy: designing your own life

One woman in her late twenties describes how she came to realize that her own experience is more valid than any predetermined, predefined life-style:

"I started relationships when I was fourteen and have been in them until last year when I turned twenty-eight. They've never lasted more than about a year, and they always overlapped. Most of the guys wanted a girl on their arm to squire around, to make them feel like a king. I guess I was looking for a sort of identity—though it took me a few years to figure this meant that I thought I was not worthy enough on my own, that I only really existed if I had a boyfriend. It was odd, because I was well-educated and knew about feminist issues, but for some reason I never applied them to myself.

"Well, once I did, it was like a volcano exploding. It was a revelation. *I did not need to be attached to a man to be a full person!* I made a commitment to myself: I would stay out of relationships for a year until I could be clear about what I wanted in a relationship, or whether I wanted one at all. I would develop my life and fill it with all the things I love, and nothing that I did not. I would not compromise. I would not spend time with people I didn't like, or do things I didn't want to do (except go to work on some mornings when I would rather sleep!). I took up riding again, I read a lot more. I worked on being much healthier physically.

"Well, one year has turned into two, and today I can hardly remember myself before: a person who was not true to herself, trapped somehow. Loneliness was a feeling I used to have when I was in those lousy relationships, but I'm virtually never lonely today. I spend a lot of time with great friends. I go out on dates and have sex once in a while.

"Sometimes I worry about being alone forever, but then I realize that this is just my old way of thinking. If my life continued this way indefinitely, that would be fine with me!"

Today, most women—while they may love men—also love the way they can live on their own. They love the way they can run their lives, pay attention to their jobs, their friends, themselves, the way they can think freely about how they can create their own lives!

Our Future. Ourselves

So far, we have seen that being single does not necessarily mean you are alone; in fact many women find that in some ways they are *more* connected to others and to the world when living on their own. But supposing being single means you *are* often alone? Is that bad? What is the great fear that seems to surround the word "alone"?

In relationships or not, most women love to spend time alone, have the luxury of time for themselves. When asked, "What do you most like to do for yourself?" most women chose activities that were done alone, such as taking a bath, reading a book, going for a long walk, sitting down and having a cup of tea, or almost anything solo. Why?

This brings up a very profound point: given the enormous social pressures on us to express only limited parts of ourselves with others, it isn't surprising that women love their moments of solitude. Many women say that they can be more themselves when they are alone than at any other time. They say being alone is not "sad" or "bad," but very refreshing and restoring to the spirit. Time spent on their own, they say, allows feelings to come to the surface which are unclear, and enables a recentering process to take place. It also allows time for creativity and planning, dreaming for the future. And what will that future be?

There are two futures we speak of here: your own personal future and the shared future as women—the future of our society, our world.

What this woman says is true both for her personally, and probably for us all:

"Being single is a time I take quantum leaps in self-development. It seems to release a surge of creative energy in me. I think I am a better person for the time I spend alone."

Perhaps it truly *is* a new time in history for women. If we can ignore and get beyond the heavy social pressures on us (and if our financial situation is not too difficult), then for the first time we can make our lives anything we want.

Finally, one woman in her fifties describes memorably her experience of being single, how she has re-created her entire life, and who she is today:

"I was a wife and mother for twenty-five years, my work was basically homemaking. My greatest achievement is my two years of college. I didn't graduate, but I still see it as my greatest achievement, beyond mothering . . . beyond anything else. I don't feel I was in the world or in any way in charge of my own life until I got divorced.

"The approximate total income of my household is about $12,000. [sic] The best job I could get when I left the marriage was as a cleaning woman—that's my experience, what I did for twenty-five years. It's worth it to be on my own. Being in control of my life. Absolute independence. I love doing what I want to do, being with who I want to be with, staying out as late as I want, changing my mind if I want, living the way I want, listening to the music I want.

"I could never really communicate with my husband, never share with him. The divorce was like death and rebirth. I felt relieved that I could start living again. I still feel relief nine years later.

"What is my sex life like? Sometimes there is no sex life.

But I enjoy periods of no sex as well as sex or being sexual by myself. I relate more aggressively the older I get. I used to be strictly heterosexual, now I get a great deal of pleasure making love to women occasionally too. But my most important relationship with a woman was nonsexual, my relationship with my daughter. She is my best friend. She is a ray of light in my life. I love her dearly.

"To women I say—you can be who you want to be. Look how I've changed! I've revised, I'm like T. S. Eliot. There will be time for a hundred more revisions. Oh, a thousand revisions."*

What more could we possibly add? She has said it all. There will be time for revisions, time for a thousand revisions for all of us. The nineties and the next century offer great possibilities for change for women. Relying on our own experience will release a surge of energy and ideas for the reorganization of society. Join in! We need you!

---

* From the 3rd HR, published as *Women and Love: A Cultural Revolution In Progress*, Alfred A. Knopf, 1987.

7

Women as Friends, Women as Lovers

We have been talking almost exclusively about relationships with men in this book, because we are trying to unravel problems in the heterosexual emotional contract to make way for a new type of life in the future. But a large component of our private lives is our relationship with other women—whether as friends or as lovers. What are relationships between women like? And is a love relationship with a woman an option for you?

Most women describe their friendships with other women as very happy and important to them. Women rely on each other, being alternately children, mothers, sisters, and friends to one another—sometimes all on the same day! There are moments of letdown, of course, and even betrayal, as in any relationship, but these tend to be the exception, not the rule.

Women Love Their Women Friends

When asked, "Who is your best friend? What do you think of her? How do you feel when you are together?" women often describe relationships full of beauty, strength, learning, and powerful emotional attachment:

"I have a sense of owning the world when we are together, a feeling of oneness: not in a romantic sense, but I feel anchored to the planet. Anything is possible with our friendship backing me up! I also find her hilariously funny. That usually results in a lighthearted feeling when I leave her. Most of all, I feel I am OK, that all is well. Nurtured."

"I always feel great after I see her. We talk about everything that's going on in our lives. It seems that she is the only person with whom I can talk about absolutely anything. She makes me feel better than anyone. If I could only have a relationship with a man that even came close to our friendship, I would be totally happy."

"We have been friends for thirteen years. She's smart, she knows me like a book, I can never fool her. She makes me aware of things about myself I don't even realize, she makes me think but won't solve my problems for me. When we are together we talk for hours. I feel like there is a strong bond between us."

One woman, in loving detail, draws a portrait of her best friend:

"Jen is my oldest and dearest friend. She has style, and most people think she is adorable to look at. She is sexy, funny, and very bright. We have been through a lifetime together. Sometimes I marvel at the length of time we have known each other, and also at the amount that has happened in both of our lives, together and apart. I marvel at the peaks and valleys of our friendship, although the valleys were never that low, only little 'glitches' caused, primarily, by distance. But we have always come together again, and I have never wavered from undying loyalty and true respect.

"We met when we were thirteen, at school. I don't remember our first meeting, but by the time half the year was over, we were fast friends, spending the night at each other's homes and swooning over our favorite pinups. We were from different backgrounds, but cut from the same cloth. We would spend hours in hysterics over something funny one of us said, a funny thought or comment.

"The first party I ever went to where there were boys, Jen was with me. We look a lot of time (weeks) deciding what to wear, and she spent a whole afternoon taking the rhinestones off a shirt I wanted to wear that night, just because I didn't like the rhinestones. I remember to this day how much that little thing meant to me.

"As we got older, we started to hang out as a group, she with her boyfriend, me with mine—the boyfriends were best friends, so we were together all the time, which was great because that is what we wanted anyway! We both were already aware of the injustices one suffered as a woman, being defined by men as sexual toys, then being put down for the same definition. We were always battling against that. But we had fun anyway, partied together, went through pain over men together, shared our deepest secrets and truths with each other. We were inseparable.

"When I went away to college, she and I had some problems at first. My whole life changed, I adopted a new vocabulary, new attitudes, made new kinds of friends. I can imagine how threatening it was for her to receive letters from someone who said she was me, but who sounded totally different! But when I went home at Christmas, we talked it out. One thing I really love about Jen is she never hesitates to speak her mind. I have never been as good at that, but the amount of it that I do, I owe to her—she showed me. She has a very strong character, and I love her for it.

"Since then we have lived in two different countries. I

think about her on almost a daily basis. Our friendship has now lasted for seventeen years. It is hard to describe how I feel about her, beyond the story I have just told. Her courage, discipline, sense of abandon, sense of humor, loyalty, ability to love, sense of her own high self-worth, her triumphs over family, work and relationship problems, her ability to see the best side of a situation, her help in guiding me when I don't know which way to turn, her undying tribute to me by calling me her best friend—all of these things are why I love her. I would love her even if she behaved like a total jerk. It is a nonrefundable love, an acceptance of her as a friend for life. We have both gotten married in the last few years, so have yet another thing to share. We all really like each other. Her husband is a doll, and so is mine. Last year they had a beautiful daughter and asked us to be godparents. What could be better than that?"

Most women speak very enthusiastically about their women friends, describing a special connection they rarely find with men—a high level of understanding, great verbal communication, and a deep caring and loyalty that survives changes and upheavals: distance, breakups, deaths. Although these are intense relationships, the conflicts are relatively infrequent and can usually be overcome.

Emotional closeness

So often women say they wish they could communicate with the men in their lives the way they communicate with their friends; women seem to "know" them, without driving them crazy with difficult and ambiguous communication and emotional barriers:

"When I really need to talk on an emotional level, really let someone into my heart, it's always easier and more rewarding with my best friend. My boyfriend doesn't seem to like to talk like this, it makes him uncomfortable. I like to know I can laugh, cry or whatever, and that anything I say is acceptable. I wish I could have this with him."

"I can talk to her about anything. There's no ego and false pride involved like there is with most men I know. I hardly ever feel satisfied after a conversation with a man the way I do when I've talked to her, or to any woman actually."

"Men tend to reduce the world and its parts to mechanical pieces. They don't see life as a whole. Women have more of an overview and see things as they relate to each other, not in isolated pieces. I go to women when I need advice, even women I don't know really well. Once when I had a big decision to make about a relationship and my best friend was away, I just blurted out all these feelings to a woman I'd just met. She was so calm and so interested. She didn't try to *tell* me what to do, she just listened and gave me feedback. Her genuine concern and empathy really came through and supported me, it helped me trust myself."

Women say that their conversations with other women are more detailed, more involved in searching out, listening for, and hearing the other's inner thoughts, working together to explore the feelings one person is trying to express. They lament the fact that men often seem to work against them in this endeavor, leaving women feeling as though they are swimming upstream. One woman analyzes it like this:

"Men I have loved seem so closed compared to women I have known. It seems as though they have such a hard time being open—I suppose they're just more cut off from their feelings. They think demonstrating such a range of feelings is 'soft' or 'weak.' It's hard to relate to a person like that. It's a great quality at the office, it 'gets things done,' but at home I don't want it."

On the whole, women do not end up feeling drained in their friendships with women, in the way they often do with men, because the emotional support is mutual: neither is giving but not receiving understanding and love.

Is it harder for most women to talk to a male lover because there is more vulnerability between lovers than friends? Or is it easier to talk to women because they are less competitive, have a different style of relating, and prefer to be supportive? While it is true that love relationships can be more intense and demanding than friendships, most men also say that the people they feel are the easiest to talk to are their women friends or their wives. Since both women and men find it easier to talk to women, it is clear that the way women communicate is preferable—the loving and nurturing way.

Women's Way of Relating: The Four Gifts

What are the skills that both women and men find so attractive? Women say that their friendships with other women are open and spontaneous, that it is easy to talk, that their women friends are good at listening and giving advice, rarely judgmental—and rarely pressure them to conform to any predefined pattern or put them down if they do not do so.

Emotional support, no questions asked

One of the greatest gifts women give each other is the knowledge that they are there for each other as emotional supports, and that no judgments will be made. This level of acceptance is the foundation of many friendships: it creates a feeling of safety that makes it possible to be open and to express oneself freely.

Women usually say they can speak more freely and honestly with each other than with men, who may refuse to talk, or may criticize them for what they are saying:

"I know that I can tell her anything, and she will never react by saying, 'God, I can't believe you *said* that, how can you *feel* such a thing? That's ridiculous!' I've had many men say that to me."

"My sister and I can talk about anything, no matter how intimate or shocking. That's because she always listens and she never judges me—she only offers loving support."

"No matter how long it's been since I've seen my woman friends, we click and can talk about anything. They're nonjudgmental, supportive, and I know if I need them they'll be there. My secrets are safe with them and they'll be honest with me."

"I'll never forget the first time I opened myself up to this older woman who is very close to me. It was at the beginning of our friendship, which has grown into one where she is my emotional mentor. I told her some deep, dark secrets about myself, things that I had never told any-one. I was shaking, but I had a feeling that she would be able to understand me. When I said each thing, I checked her face and she didn't look shocked at all. All she said was, 'I'm so glad you told me that, that you feel safe enough with me to share this way. It means a lot to me.' I couldn't believe that she was thanking *me* for such a valu-able gift *she* had given. This acceptance of me changed my life, my relating to others, my sense of self-worth."

Listening—with genuine interest

Often women enthusiastically praise the way their friends show interest in hearing their thoughts and experi-ences:

"When I talk with my women friends, I know they are *really* listening and concentrating on what I have to say, whether it is an important thing or a little thing. It spoils me, though, for in the outside world men don't listen the same way, and I am always surprised (one more time) when they don't. Why can't they be this respectful?"

"When we talk, she really is interested in what I say. What I think about things, what I do with my day, people I meet, they are all interesting to her. She is curious about all the things I do, and her interest is respectful, exciting, loving—I know she wants the best for me. She helps me when I am making a decision, and gives me a feeling of validity, which makes me feel like everything I do in my life is important."

"My friend is beautiful and talented, although she prob-ably wouldn't admit it. She has done some amazing things with her life, has come a long way from when I first met her. I was her support in the beginning of our friendship, but it has turned into a two-way street. Now, when I am feeling bad, I can call her and she will completely identify with whatever it is I am going through, even if she hasn't gone through it herself. She has an outstanding ability to empathize. It means so much to me. When I call her, at home or at work, I always get off the phone feeling warmer, more supported, more strong. I love her very much."

Constructive criticism and ideas

Women say that the kind of support they receive from their women friends often results in enlightenment or learning. Their friends may tell them when they've made a mistake, help them to overcome destructive habits, or help them to remove themselves from situations that they might not see are bad for them. Yet this advice is easy to take because it so clearly comes with a sense of love and loyalty:

"At first, her constant comments about the relationship I was in annoyed me. She was always saying that I deserved something more and that I didn't need to put up with this any longer. She was right. But I resented it, I thought she was criticizing me. I didn't see that it hurt her to see me in so much pain. The time had long passed where I was getting enough from this man to make it worth staying—I wasn't. Finally, I started to notice that, although she criticized him for hurting me and criticized me, albeit gently, for staying with him, she never told me I was unacceptable. In fact, she said that she could remember being where I was before. When I realized this, I valued her even more. Her advice was sound. She was right."

Another woman describes how her best friend has always been there for her, giving criticism and love:

"We have been close friends for about two and a half years. There are a lot of things about us that are the same, and a lot of things that are different. From the beginning, we have shared everything on a very deep emotional level. First it was just talking, now it means pouring out our hearts to each other, letting each other see our vulnerabilities and our tears.

"I went through a devastating breakup about two years ago, and she was there for me every step of the way. When she thought I was being self-destructive, she told me so and helped me discover new ways of 'being.' When I needed comfort, she was there with lots of it. We lived around the corner from each other, and I spent nearly all my waking hours with her, sometimes talking, sometimes just eating and watching the TV in the quiet. Because of her constancy and support, I was able to go through that experience. I am a better person for it, and a better person for sharing friendship with her. Now, we live in different cities, but I still feel as close, and we are still there for each other, we call each other for reassurance and love when we need it. She will be my maid of honor when I marry this summer. I can't describe what this relationship means to me. It means closeness and intimacy, support and strength. It means everything."

Courage in times of trouble

How often have women been each other's support in times of difficulty? In the nineteenth century and earlier, women were generally the ones who helped each other during childbirth, acting as midwives and coaches. When women need a helping hand, a baby-sitter, someone to lean on, a place to stay, more often than not it is another woman who is there.

Who would you call in a crisis? Women often know what to do:

"I had a friend in college who was very attractive, very bright and very Catholic. She was popular, she worked hard and did not get caught up in as much of the wild partying as I did. When I found out I was pregnant, I was devastated. I knew what I had to do, but I didn't want to go alone. When I called her, there wasn't a moment of discomfort between us. Straight away, she called the clinic, made an appointment for the next morning, then she came over, fixed dinner, and spent the night with me. She never once let it show that my decision to have an abortion offended her. She just put that aside for me. I was so impressed by her loyalty and steadfastness and her ability to make me feel accepted for what I was doing, and for taking charge at a time when I simply couldn't. I will never forget how she helped me, and what it meant to me."

Lamentably, these four gifts of women's friendship are undervalued by society. Both women and men seek them out and enjoy them, but rather than being praised for these qualities, for their well-developed emotional literacy and ability to relate, women are labeled negatively as "too loving," "overemotional" and so on. Where are the positive stereotypes of women's virtues?

Importantly, in a historic sense, many women are trying to repress these qualities. They are under great pressure from society—at work, for example—to be "more like a man": "control your feelings," don't talk "too much," develop "male" gestures. Other women are fighting this type of pressure, refusing to wear "masculine" business suits if they don't want to, refusing to try to be "one of the guys" on the job. If women who act more like men are rewarded with advancement and higher pay, who can blame women for trying to modify their behavior? And yet, won't we all be much less well off if women are no longer there with their traditional warmth and support? Isn't the answer that more men should learn to be more loving and open, less harshly competitive?

We need to change the basic value structure of society so that empathy and a desire for the common good are valued over aggression and warlike qualities. Such a change could cure many things that are wrong with our society, such as the exploitation of the environment. Men's dominating, exploitative attitude toward women is mirrored in our society's attitude toward nature; our assumption that we can use the environment for our own purposes, that we don't have to interact or show mutual respect for all forms of life is what has brought us to the current impasse.

Breaking Up with a Friend

What we have said up till now has all been positive but —surprise, surprise—friendships between women are not always perfect!

"I have found it difficult to express any anger towards her. She is so intensely sensitive that she breaks down in tears whenever I try to tell her she has made me angry, which I think is an important part of close friendship—the freedom to be honest with each other about your 'bad' as well as your 'good' feelings."

"There is nothing better than being with her when she is feeling good, it's the most satisfying time I spend with anyone. But she gets incredibly sad, and I have begun to feel frustrated by it. Nothing I say seems to help, and she doesn't come out of it very quickly. I'm just expected to go along with it and listen to her for hours and then enjoy the good times when they come."

"I am jealous of my best friend. I have never admitted it before. I feel so guilty about it. But when she spends more time with other people, I hate it and feel left out. I try *never* to let it show."

Many relationships between women *can* go through ups and downs, friendships growing closer through this. But not all problems can be solved. Some women tell sad stories of breaking up with a woman friend they loved:

"My best friend and I are kind of drifting apart right now. She wants to be a dancer and she is doing some kind of exotic dancing. Now, I've never seen her do it but I have an idea of what this is like. She is not totally nude but she doesn't wear a whole lot and she just basically dances in these bars and she gets paid pretty well for it. She likes this dancing and she knows I disapprove of it. It's really changed our friendship. I find the whole thing absolutely nauseating, the fact that men just sit there and watch her, not because she has good dancing technique, but because she is using her sexuality to get their attention."

"She has become involved in a job and a guy that are interrelated (her boss is her boyfriend), and now she doesn't have time for me. I drop by their business sometimes, but she is always too busy to talk and suggests that we get together on the weekend but then she always calls it off, has something better to do. I feel I was just a stopgap until she found what she really wanted—a man and a career. Now I'm old news. This hurts me because I came to depend on her emotionally, to need her input into my life, to express with her and to laugh with her. I feel cheated. I thought she needed me too.''

"My 'best friend' is a beautiful, brilliant woman who has been through a great deal. She has always had this awful habit of thinking the world will wait for her. Even in the seventies, when we were all hanging out she would always be late for dinner parties, or sometimes call and cancel, or sometimes not call at all and not show up. Everyone would laugh (me included) and say, 'Well, ha ha, that's her, crazy Anna.' We all worried about her constantly, about her health and well-being. She drank and smoked too much.

"The last few years she has stood me up so much I'm beginning not to be sympathetic. I have invited her to come and stay with us for a week many times. She always says she is definitely coming, but then she never does. I hid my disappointment and hurt and carried on saying the usual, 'Ah, that's Anna.' But recently it has really started to get to me. I would never treat anyone that way.

"I think the final straw came when I invited her for this New Year's Eve. I was excited she was coming because she lives so far away and we spend so little time together. I made reservations at a fabulous restaurant (at her suggestion) and went shopping for special foods for her (she is vegetarian). She called the day before and said, 'Sorry, love, but I'm with friends up in the country and I can't seem to get anyone to take me to where you are.' She blamed it on everyone else.

"When I hung up, all the disappointment of the past eighteen years welled up in me. I am in the process of

writing her a letter saying that I can no longer accept
friendship on this basis."

Attraction to Other Women

Shyness: how to handle it

Don't friendships sometimes border on being "in love"?
If we feel so enthusiastic about another woman, aren't we
"in love" a little bit? Can we tell the other person? Is it
necessary? What would we say?

In general, there is no vocabulary for such feelings of
attraction between women who do not want to have a les-
bian relationship, but who nevertheless want to express the
intensity of their friendship in some way. How do women
deal with these feelings? What are the choices?

In Victorian times, women's letters and diaries show that
women spoke and wrote to each other much more inti-
mately, using such phrases as, "my dearest one," "when I
am with you, my heart sings," or, remembering their time
together, "your warmth was everywhere." These are not
unusual phrases; they were commonplace and appear over
and over again in women's documents of the period. Also,
it was quite customary for women to walk in the street
together arm in arm, or hand in hand. This was not considered in any way strange or unusual, just a sign of friendship. Today this heritage lingers in the customary kiss on
the cheek women are "allowed" to give each other on
arriving and departing (as long as they take care to keep
their bodies in an A-frame position, so that areas below the
neck never meet!).

How did our physicality become so straitjacketed that
now anyone we touch for more than a minute must be a

"lover"? That the only sustained physical warmth we can get is from someone we have sex with? The line between polite treatment of a friend and physical intimacy has become too hard and fast.

Why is it that with a friend we have known and loved for ten years or more we cannot sit cuddled up together watching television? While this might just be possible while we are still in school, it becomes less and less "acceptable" as we get older. Married women in particular are supposed to become the "property" of the man in the marriage; remnants of this idea are to be found in the feeling (discussed in chapter 5) that we cannot talk about the deeper parts of what goes on in a relationship with our friends because this would show a lack of "loyalty" to our men.

There is certainly nothing wrong with using words we normally reserve for a lover in speaking to a friend, if this is how we feel. Physical warmth and intimacy between friends should be possible, not every physical gesture should be seen as some "preliminary" to sex. But who will be the first to initiate such brave gestures?

When friendship becomes sexual

However, one woman tells how, while in a difficult heterosexual relationship, she found herself gradually falling in love with a woman friend:

"The best relationship I have ever had was with a woman. A friendship that developed quickly evolved, slowly, into intimacy. I was living with an intolerable man at the time, someone who would play cruel games with me and even hurt me physically. It was a tumultuous five years, filled with jealousy and distrust.

"I met her at work. It was instant 'like'—not physical,

but a connection we couldn't deny. Gradually, I found myself wanting to be with her more than I wanted to be with him. I felt warm, valued and safe with her; with him I only felt hollow and a deep sense of lack. Everything I wanted in a relationship I was receiving from her: nurturing, respect, validation, and trust. He was stifling and suffocating, she delighted in my self-expansion. For the first time in my life, I was free to be who I am.

"Within a year, it just happened . . . that first kiss. I don't know if it was the secrecy of it, or the excitement of doing something that is viewed as 'wrong,' but it was so full of feeling . . . I was exhilarated. It felt so natural. There was no shame. It was new for both of us, but it felt so right. Eventually, I left him and moved in with her."

Another woman, who has had relationships with men and women, describes why she prefers women. The differences she finds in communication and level of intensity are the reasons she gave:

"The conversations with Anne-Marie would be so complete and involved. For instance, 'Oh, this dinner we're going to, I have really mixed feelings about it. How do you feel about it?' And then we would speculate on our thoughts, talk about it. Or if we were having a fight, one of us might say, 'You're really taking advantage of me,' and then the other would say, 'Tell me why—explain to me how you feel about that—tell me what you mean, in depth.' Then she would listen to me for five or ten minutes. She might complain about what I said, but still she would listen. That's the relationship I had with her.

"With a woman in a relationship, nothing's taken for granted, whereas men sometimes have the attitude: we'll just cruise along here, and everything will be OK. With women, there's always a discussion, always, and the direction of the relationship is constantly up for revision. At least, it's like that with us. Whereas in an argument or a discussion with my ex-boyfriend, I would get—nothing. It would just be totally disregarded. Or if I pushed, he would say, 'You're crazy, I just refuse to discuss this.' And that would be the end of the conversation. I would rant and rave, on and on, without him listening, without him paying a bit of attention to me—he would usually start doing something else at the same time, like cleaning his desk. And then after I had done ranting and raving, he would say, 'See what I mean? You're a complete lunatic.' And he'd walk away and not say anything else.

"I definitely get more response from my woman lover. Talking with her is completely different. (Of course, it depends on how patient we are that day with each other.) But more often than not, when I bring up something, or drop a remark, the response I get is, 'What do you mean? How can you say that?' or, 'Tell me more about what you meant by that.'

"On the other hand, sometimes with my previous woman lover it all became such a complex psychological interaction, it became topheavy. Anything you do you know can be interpreted in thousands of ways by the other person, and to discuss it becomes a massive thing. During one of these discussions, in fact, my previous girlfriend just told me to fuck off. She just couldn't deal with so much analyzing of feelings, there was too much intensity and focus on the relationship for her.

"Of course, it's true, to a degree, when you have two women who are telling each other all their inner thoughts, both very intense, it can get really turned inward—but still, it's great. I think that your identity develops through these discussions. It's a real process of discovery for me—both of me and of her. It's a great experience."

Loving Another Woman

Of course, love between women does involve many of the same human problems women face in heterosexual relationships, because we are all vulnerable to being hurt when we are in love. But there is still a feeling that love between women often *is* simpler and *does* work better—and for many it is more serious, on a different plane:

"Falling in love is not as important as not falling in love. These relationships I share with women with whom I am forever in love—with, or probably without, sex—are the relationships I value above all others. The lovers who are closer than friends; friends deeper and more multifaceted than lovers. The ones I will always meet up with again, and know they are somewhere out there in the world, not forgetting our love, using it to strengthen them."

"I believe a love relationship between two women is far more serious than one between a man and a woman. Women run on a higher emotional level than men will let themselves, and they get to deeper levels with each other."

Is love between women more equal? Seeing what other women have said here about the differences in style between communicating with women and with men, it would seem that the answer is yes—these relationships are more equal, and conducted in a different way.

Gay women's descriptions of their lives with their lovers are often filled with warmth and jubilance, when they talk about the kinds of things they like to do together:

"I love being a woman and being gay. Nearly all my friends are gay women. I have a lover now, and we have an exciting although turbulent relationship. It's not all roses by any means! But it feels good and she sparks my imagination. I think I love her."

"Laughing, talking, drinking, eating, discussing—we make love through all of it. We're passionate in different ways all day. It's wonderful and fun being together."

"I want to do everything there is to do with her, and see all there is to see. There is nothing I do that I would not rather have her share with me than do alone. We love to go to parties together, walk in the park, play softball, take hot baths, and make love. We also love reading to each other. But, mostly, I just love to wake up in the morning and look over at her and know that she loves me. It's the best!"

One older gay woman describes how she feels about her life, and warmly describes her large circle of friends, many of whom are ex-lovers:

"I'm gay, been gay all my life, have many friends and ex-lovers who are friends, and a large circle of women I am close to. I have always loved being gay. Being accepted as an equal among equals. I think women are wonderful, I just love women, I always have. Most of my life, I have been in long relationships. I went with one woman for ten years, and another for seven. Those were the longest, but it was always four years, three years—things like that. I was always going with somebody . . . There was a woman I really loved—she was very, very good-looking and rich (maybe not too bright). We had a strong sexual alliance—

the physical relationship was just sublime. I melted when I saw her, I forgot where I was and who I was in her arms. I floated away to some other world . . .

"If I could generalize in the abstract, women are more caring. Of course, I am a woman, so it's easier for me to relate to women. I think they're nicer people. Besides, I like dealing with equals, with peers. I like people who are like me . . . I like the way women look and smell. And feel. They feel and smell and look better than men do. They even sound better. I like everything they do better.

"I just love living. I like what I do. I like socializing. I love going to the movies. I love reading books. I love being alone. I love watching my VCR. I love going to parties. I love dancing. I love walking my dog. I love the beach. I get a lot of pleasure out of life. I just love the things I do."

Sex between women

Gay women describe very multifaceted types of sex with each other:

"When we make love, both of us assume different roles all the time—during one night, we might roll around, one on top of the other at different times, one taking charge one minute, the other taking charge the next. It is sexy, but it is also a statement of the way we are together—no one is in control more than the other. We lie in each other's arms, smell each other's breath and the scent of our bodies mingles together. I feel a calm and deep passion afterwards, like I have been made whole. It is nothing like sex I ever had with men."

"My sex life now is happy, joyful and fulfilling—actual sex play to orgasm happens only about once a week, but

the touching, snuggling, and holding is at least as important and that's every day. Sex is like dessert —a treat when
we have the time or are in the mood—wonderful, but not
the core of our love."

"I feel desired when she makes love to me. I also feel
she recognizes my vulnerability and is treating me gently."

"I like rough, passionate sex because it goes beyond the
barriers of 'niceness' that so many women build around
themselves. There's no feeling of holding back, as there so
often is with politically correct, gentle sex."

What does it mean to love another woman?

Who is to say which is more "natural": to love the opposite sex or one's own? In ancient Greece men would have
been hard-pressed to answer that—they frequently had
male lovers *and* wives!

Many women here have expressed the deepest feelings
of love, joy, passion, and sorrow for the women they love,
either just as friends or as friends and lovers. At one level
or another, all of us have the chance to share in the beauty
of women, the power of womanhood.

The Problems and Politics of Women's Friendships

We may love our women friends, but how seriously do
we take them? Do we really think they are as important as
men? As capable of filling a seat in government? Of flying

an airliner? Of running a major corporation? Or, even, of thinking rationally?

Although women praise their friends and obviously love them, these friendships often exist outside the power relationships of jobs, families, and so on. Our love for each other is almost "outside" society in a way, not a part of the "real" world.

How many of us think that since men run the world and have more money and power, they are more important? We may not want to think like this, but on some level, it appears that we do. One of the ways this lack of respect for women shows is in the casual way some women will still cancel plans with another woman if a man asks them out.

When women put men first: canceling appointments

Many women have felt hurt by the way their friends take the men in their lives more seriously:

"I have been canceled at short notice by my friends when a guy calls them up, maybe on the very day we were supposed to be going out. It's sort of the 'girl's code' but it really pisses me off. I resent being considered less important, being taken for granted. I would never do that to another woman."

"She always waits for me to call *her* now, and never makes plans for us to spend time together anymore. I guess that once you have a guy or get married, everything is different."

"I remember once canceling an arrangement with a woman because I had had yet another huge fight with my boyfriend and he had called and said he wanted to have dinner with me. She got angry and said, 'It seems you take your relationship with him more seriously than your relationship with me!' This upset me a lot, and I spent some time defending myself in my head about it. But eventually, I realized she was right. I think it was insulting to her, a kind of attitude I don't want to have. Now I think it is reprehensible to put men first. My women friends are very important to me. Commitments made to them are just as significant as commitments made to my boyfriends."

Do we spend too much time talking about men?

While most women enjoy telling and hearing from their friends what is going on in their relationships with men, some think that to talk too much about men is just using each other—as if the basis of the friendship is a mutual sympathy society over men, rather than a real interest in each other:

"What I've always disliked about women friends is their constant talk about their involvements with men. It bothered me that we didn't talk enough about our *own* plans and problems."

"It has hurt me in the past when I felt my only place in her life was to talk about the men she was going out with. There ought to be more going on in a friendship than just talking about guys and what they do to you, how they make you feel."

"Probably one of the most tiring parts of my being with women friends is that so many of them are continually talking about men. I get tired of discussing whether there are any 'good men' around. There is more to single life than finding a man! I tell them, 'Who cares?' "

"I've disliked women friends who constantly talked about their relationships with men; *we* talked about what they should have been talking to the *man* about."

But most women do not feel this way; most say that these conversations are extremely important because they enable them to think through how they feel about what a man is doing, to reaffirm their own value system:

"I never could have survived this relationship and left him without her constant support and always being available to listen to me crying and babbling. She was solid, humorous and kind. Without her to bounce my feelings off, I would never have got to the truer, deeper ones, the ones that were buried for so long."

Is spending a lot of time talking about men "using" women friends? Or is it part of working out a philosophy of life?

Far from being "silly girl talk," these conversations are extremely important. Also, they are often highly philosophical: through discussing particular situations and trying to decipher together a man's assumptions about women and "love" (How does he actually feel? Why does he behave as he does?), women clarify their own feelings about what is going on, see the situation more clearly, and think more lucidly about what they want their responses to be. These conversations help women evolve a sophisticated set of values, "women's ways of being."

Most women say that comparing notes like this helps them sort out whether they are getting what they really want from a relationship, and also keeps them emotionally afloat, avoiding the isolation that can occur in a problematic relationship (see chapter 5).

The situations many women discuss with each other relate to the emotional violence we defined in chapter 1. In these conversations, women hear and acknowledge what other women, their friends, are experiencing. This is especially important because society denies that these patterns of attempted emotional and psychological domination exist. Without digging them out and looking at them with someone else, women would have to accept what society teaches: that if there are problems, they are the *woman's* fault, she should readjust her view of things, or possibly go to a psychiatrist if the problems persist. While talking to a psychoanalyst or counselor can be helpful at times, many do not acknowledge that the status of women, and men's assumptions about them, are a large-scale social problem, which makes relationships difficult. This needs to be considered when discussing what is going on. So the help women get from their friends in figuring out how to deal with various stereotypes is enormously important.

Fear of Other Women

Jealousy and envy

What about the old cliché that women are bitchy and jealous toward each other? It is less true today? Was it ever true?

Some women can bring themselves to talk, usually guiltily, about those "old-fashioned" feelings of jealousy—usually envy, or a fear of being left out:

"My friend Ellen is prettier than me. I wish that I did not feel threatened by that. I tell myself to be self-confident, I promise myself that I will applaud her for her physical beauty, but when she walks in, in a knockout dress, all confidence and smiles, it's all over. I try to pick her apart in my mind, and can't wait to discover a flaw! It's terrible. Theoretically, I want to encourage attractive women like her to be part of our circle of friends, and to not be afraid for her to be friends with my boyfriend. Do I have to see every pretty woman as a threat? But I do! I suppose I am all for the empowerment of women—except for women who are more attractive than me! What a hypocrite I am."

"My boss is beautiful, rich, and powerful. I am insanely jealous, it is just too much! I hate her, I want to *be* her. But I never let it show, because I know that would make me look a wimp. I *am* a wimp. Why can't I get over this? It makes it worse that on top of it all I *like* her so much."

"I was on holiday in a place where there are nude beaches. I felt jealous and threatened by the women there because I was worried the man I was with would think they were sexier, and had better shapes. But if I'd been alone, I probably would have still said to myself, 'Why can't I look like that?' Or 'Why can't I be so nonchalant in the nude?' I didn't feel trust in these women, and I never tried to make friends with them. I would like myself better if I wasn't so threatened by them."

One woman describes conquering these feelings of jealousy:

"I used to feel very jealous of my best friend, although I hid and covered it over. She always seemed more together, more attractive to me and more in charge of her life. I decided to tell her how I felt, hoping this might dissipate the fears. It was a risk, but I thought, What the hell, I can't stand feeling this way, it's too painful. What can I lose? And I really wanted to be friends with her. When I told her, she was surprised and very warm. She told me all the things about herself that she didn't like, her looks and personality. She told me how envious she was of parts of my personality and my legs! After she let me in on her insecurities, I felt so much stronger. Since then she asks me for reassurance just as much as I ask her. Now I don't look at her in the same way."

Feeling insecure with women

Will other women criticize us, we sometimes fear, like our mothers may have done? After all, for most of us, it was our mother who had the job of supervising us, disciplining us, teaching us, and so our mother was more apt to criticize as well as encourage. This criticism from one so powerful could have felt very painful, and seems to limit our ability to be free, to create our own identity.

The result is that some women, like men, have an instinctive fear of other women, expecting the worst. This is very prevalent, even though our relationships with women —especially at work, for instance—are often good on the surface. We can be too quick to bail out when we hear any negative words from a woman, much quicker than when we hear criticism or condescension from a man.

Is it possible that we, like men, have a love-hate relationship with women? That we, like men, don't respect other women as much as we do men? And this implies, of course, that we do not respect ourselves as much, either. If this is true, it is a sad state of affairs. This is something we must face and deal with; not to do so means we will be destined to repeat ourselves, we will perpetuate the same negative stereotypes about women we deplore so much when they are used against us. We ourselves will hold each other back.

If we believed in each other, we could do anything. After all, we are over 51 percent of the population. Why can't we unite, and at least elect people who make certain women receive equal pay with men?

Torn Allegiances

The reason we don't have solidarity is not because we are "naturally jealous," but because we don't really think highly enough of other women—yet. And we aren't fully aware of this—yet.

For example, one woman, studying to be a lawyer, was heard saying, "I don't want to be referred to as a woman lawyer when I graduate, but as a person." It is quite understandable that she does not want to be discriminated against because she is a woman, pointed out as "different." On the other hand, there is something else involved here. Men do not mind being classed as "men," in fact, being a man, a Real Man, is something most men are proud of and want very much to achieve. But for many women, who have internalized the general view of society that women are less, being classified as a woman reeks of social disapproval.

Of course, it would be ideal if society did not focus so much on gender and we did not have this problem to deal with. But it does classify us from birth on every form we fill in thereafter; even in the way we are addressed: Mr. and Ms. Since this is the reality we live with, we must, it seems, take a stand regarding our own category. Why not be proud of our identity, proud of what women have achieved? There are many books that celebrate women's past, present, and future, even though women's contributions are trivialized or discounted in most history textbooks—and in many contemporary newspapers.

The situation for women is not dissimilar to that of African Americans. A few years ago, African Americans were seen by so many as second-class citizens. They still receive terribly unequal treatment, but due to a painfully slow shift in consciousness, they are gradually turning the world's view around, hopefully more and more each day.

Do we think men are more important?

This phenomenon of not really respecting ourselves or other women—even though we may love them—comes out frequently in women's statements about their mothers. Surprisingly, the majority of women say they grew up feeling closer to their father than their mother—that they admired him more, wanted to be more like him, not at all like their mothers:

"I identify more with my father because he always had a job and I do too. I want to be more like him than I want to be like my mother. But my mother I can talk to in a way I never could with my father. She is always there for me— not on every level, but for bottom-line survival, I know she is there. She is the one I turn to when I've got to be *sure.*"

"My mother is a beautiful, kind, intelligent woman. I love her very much, but I can say that I don't admire her much. She has limited her life. I know that being free means being able to choose any life you want, but that's not why she never left the house. She did it because she had no ambition and my father didn't want her to."

This identification derives from the fact that our fathers tended to have a higher status than our mothers, were usually more important "in the world," had more money, were more exciting, and perhaps had more time to play with us, since they were not involved in housework. But once again, what we see being internalized here is the idea that women are *less*—less desirable, less fun, less interesting, and so on.

This is a frequently unexamined part of our relationship with our mothers—and ourselves—although when women see their women friends behave as though men are superior, they recognize this behavior for what it is and often remark that it hurts them.

Fear of male power

Another way this comes out is that women frequently say they notice how much their friends diminish themselves in men's company—that they are afraid to express their thoughts or may withdraw a remark immediately if there is any sign of male disapproval—becoming true wimps, in fact!

"My friend has such strong opinions, I really love it when she gets going. But put her around a man and she becomes this demure little thing, nodding in agreement. It makes me furious."

"I admire women who can love other women and not be ingratiating with men. I hate women who have split personalities—one for their women friends and one for their men friends. I admire a woman who loves who she is and doesn't try to live up to someone else's expectations."

One woman describes how she first noticed this wimpy tendency in herself, then stopped herself from behaving in this way:

"I realized one day that I had always felt frustrated and denied when I was in social situations with men, but it had always been a vague feeling. Then I realized that one of the reasons was I didn't really act like who I am with them. It's hard to explain, but somehow I knew that if I was to be who I actually am—strong, animated, and argumentative—it would turn them off. And since they were 'meant' to like me, I had to tone myself down to the point where I hardly existed. When I realized this, it was a wonderful feeling—because I also realized that I was no longer going to do this, and that was fine with me. If they didn't like it, too bad. But I was not going to be ingratiating and entertaining to men anymore when I didn't want to be."

Fear of speaking out

If we can't count on our friends in public how can we unify and change women's status? If we see them bow to "male" power, how can we respect them? It is difficult for many women to watch their friends treat men and women differently, to trust men as if they deserve more status and respect. Or to see that, even though their friends realize the injustices they suffer from the male-dominated world, they don't take any action to challenge that "authority."

Women talk about seeing these dynamics work in subtle but infuriating ways, even in everyday social situations. It can be hard for us to speak out and make our thoughts known; if a woman does voice an opinion in a mixed group, she may be told she is trying to "dominate" the situation or the men present. But if she is silent, she may be labeled "wimpy." She may be reminded by the men present (or even some women) that men dislike "aggressive" women! So what is the solution?

Obviously what *you* feel and think is as important as anything a man may feel and think. You have just as much right to say what you think as any man does, and it is at least as valuable. Of course, what stops many women is the fear of men's power. (Perhaps he is your employer?) But if we stick up for each other we can conquer that power! We must speak out without fear in all situations, overcome our intimidation, and support and defend each other as we do so, because as history shows us, groups or individuals with power don't give it up without a fight—and men clearly won't!

What do you *really* think of women?

Ask yourself these questions to discover how you *really* feel about the women in your life—your best friend, your sisters, your work colleagues, your mother:

- Who is your best friend? How do you feel about her? Emotionally? Politically?
- Do you feel guilty about things you have done to women in social or business situations? Proud?
- Do you use your friends' emotional availability and nurturing as much as men use yours?

- When was the last time you phoned your friend just to say hello and ask how she is—not to cry on her shoulder?

- Are some of your women friends "less attractive" and less successful than you? Does it mean anything that they are or that they are not, or is it of no importance?

- Do you think women are silly because they spend so much money on makeup? Do you, and does it bother you? Or do you sometimes think it is fun to enjoy adornment?

- Do you ever walk down the street walking arm in arm or holding your friend's hand? How long can you do it before you become uncomfortable?

- Do you expect less from women than from men? More? Do you think they are more or less capable?

- Do you speak up when men are discriminating against women? Or do you usually try to avoid confrontation?

- If your best woman friend was looking for a position in government, would you secretly think she wasn't as capable as the man she's running against?

- Do you *really* believe that women should be half of the ruling body in your country/company/household? And would you like to be in that group?

- Would you feel as married if a woman performed the ceremony?
- Do you know the date for International Women's Day?

Women's Solidarity: The Key to Our Future

If we don't take women as seriously as we take men, we will never have the solidarity to change things.

And we *do* need to change things: the highest percentage of those living in poverty throughout the world is women and children, and this percentage is rising. A woman who divorces can expect to see her income drop sharply after the divorce; most do not receive child support. Women still earn just over half as much as men, on average, for similar work. Is this fair? Do you want to change it? Do you also want to change the emotional inequality that plagues most love relationships between women and men?

Men may have more power than we do. However, if women stick together to lobby for good basic child care, and an end to sexual discrimination in education and wages, we could change things in no time. Why is it that so many women fail to perceive or act on this? Is it because, as "second-class citizens," some women would rather identify with men? And so feel (falsely) superior?

Only if we support one another and have courage can

we make equality a reality. Without solidarity, we will have nothing except more socks to wash, more emotional unfulfillment, and increasing domestic violence, whether physical or emotional. Being proud of each other is the key to improving our status—and even our relationships with men we love!

To change things, why don't we unify and work together for goals we can all agree on—such as equal pay? And meanwhile let's make changes in our personal lives— rewrite the emotional contract we have been talking about. Insist that men work *with* us, lobby for equal rights with us. And always, always, whether it's in love or friendship, let's stick up for each other.

To believe in each other

What is the most important advice women can offer each other now?

"My advice to women? Love and respect each other, the rest will come."

"Open your eyes. Value your women friends, love yourself and each other first. Don't be afraid to be strong and define *yourself.*"

"When I was about twenty-three, I finally realized how men behaved in relationships and how much energy I put into making relationships work. I somehow stopped loving men. I feel that supporting and valuing women and putting my time and energy and love into them is the best thing I can do to change the world. I am sure that this will change men too. It will force them to question their behavior and they will start to talk to each other and give each other more emotional support. Every time a man is left by a woman, it forces him to question his behavior—at least a little bit."

"Make sure you always have a support group of women. Women are bright and strong and emotionally expressive, loving and motivated."

"If I could give any advice to other women, it would be to clear out of your life the things that make you unhappy. Don't stick with ugly jobs or ugly relationships because of some future thing you're hoping for. Don't suffer now in anticipation that it will be better in the future. Spend more time on the things that do make you happy. And love other women—don't let the system get to you! *You are great and you can make it!*"

If we continue to carry in our hearts society's prejudices about women, if we don't change things, including our own attitudes, all the work women have done recently for women's rights could be washed away: equal credit ratings at banks, the right of women to be single, the right of women not to be battered in marriage. The rape of women and physical battering are outrageous, and any human should be able to see this, yet it is only within the last few years that women, demonstrating great courage and bravery in speaking out, have managed to make these seemingly "natural" human rights important national issues.

Let's keep up the tradition. Remember, even steps toward equal pay, for example, which affect us all directly, can only be made by working together. Don't let us all down—don't let *yourself* down! Let's do it!

Many women now *do* support each other. This does not mean that all women we know are perfect, or that we ourselves are perfect, or that every woman we meet has the same nurturing and loving qualities that have been praised here. There are women, as we have seen, who still believe (to some extent) that men are "better," that women are "silly," who don't understand the importance of women's solidarity as the source of their personal strength and women's power. But probably these attitudes are becoming less.

The possibilities are enormous, if we just open our eyes: if we *look* at our women friends, we will see each other in a whole new light.

About the authors

Shere Hite graduated with a master's degree *cum laude* in history from the University of Florida then studied for her doctorate in history at Columbia University in New York. She became actively involved in the feminist movement during the 1970s, and in 1976, after five years' research, published the ground-breaking *The Hite Report on Female Sexuality.* This work was the first to document in women's own voices the reality of their sexual lives, to state explicitly that the definition of sex as 'intercourse' is socially and culturally constructed, not biologically ordained, and to create a new theory about the nature of sexuality. *The Hite Report on Female Sexuality* became an international best-seller, and later, along with *The Hite Report on Male Sexuality,* won an award for distinguished service from the American Association of Sex Educators, Counsellors and Therapists.

From 1977 to 1989 Hite travelled extensively in Europe, Asia and the United States, including those countries in which her books are banned, speaking about women's place in history and researching the final two parts of her now classic trilogy, *The Hite Report on Male Sexuality* and *The Hite Report on Women and Love. Women and Love,* based on the testimony of 4,500 women, is the first work to document the extent of entrenched emotional violence against women, and to document women themselves in the process of re-naming and redefining the cultural ideology of 'love'. Hite's view of women's thinking as 'a cultural revolution in progress' was considered highly controversial, and became an international *cause célèbre* in 1987–8, leading to the formation of a defense committee for her in 1988.

Shere Hite has taught at the University of Florida and New York University, and has received numerous honorary awards. She is listed in the 1978 *World Almanac* as one of the twenty-five most influential women in America. Hite is also well-known for her philanthropic work, and she is currently active in the ecology movement, writing a satirical novel including ecological themes.

She is married to the German classical pianist Friedrich Höricke and lives in New York.

Kate Colleran was born in New York in 1959 and grew up in England. She returned to the United States in 1977. Graduating from Smith College, Massachusetts, with a B.A. in English Literature, she has been involved in publishing and the acting world, and has worked for Shere Hite.

Kate Colleran, who is the daughter of actress Lee Remick, has travelled extensively and is now based in New York, where she lives with her husband, Pike Sullivan.

QUESTIONS FOR READERS*

Please Answer!

After you have read this book, your answers to some of the following questions would be greatly appreciated for Shere Hite's future research. The results will be published as a large-scale discussion of what was said, with many quotes.

This questionnaire is anonymous, so do not sign it. Also, it is not necessary to answer every question! Feel free to skip around and answer only those that interest you.

Statistical Information:

Age:
Under 18__ 18–24__ 25–34__ 35–44__ 45–54__ 55–68__
Over 68__

In a relationship or not:
Single, not in a relationship__ (Are you divorced?__)
Single, in a relationship__ (Are you divorced?__)
Single, living with someone__ (Are you divorced?__)
Married__ Number of years__ Children?__ At home?__

Occupation:
Student__ Manager__ Administrative/support__
Unemployed__ Professional__ Self-employed__
Manual labor/military__ Full-time mother__

Sexual orientation:
Heterosexual__ Lesbian__ Bisexual__ Celibate__

Religious Background:
Are you religious?__ Which is your religion?_____
No religion__

Nationality, race or ethnic background: _____

About You

1. Which parts of this book did you find most emotionally relevant to you *and your life now?*
2. How would you describe your general emotional state? Exuberant, pensive, depressed, tuned into work, *having fun,* etc.? How "happy" are you, on a scale of one to ten (ten is happiest)?
3. Which is more satisfying to you right now—your work or your private life?

* Copyright © 1990 Shere Hite

4. What today made you happiest?

5. How did you spend the last three New Year's Eves? How did you feel about them? What would you like to do next New Year's Eve?

What Does Love Mean to You? What is Love?

6. Are you "in love" at present?

7. When has love seemed most exciting to you (either now or in the past)? Most painful?

8. How would you define love? Is love the thing you work at in a relationship over a period of time, or is it the strong feeling you have right from the beginning?

9. When and with whom were you most deeply in love? What was it like? Did the relationship last? Why or why not?

10. When were you happiest in love for the longest period of time? Or were you happier on your own?

11. If you have ever broken up with someone important, or gotten divorced, what was it like? Who wanted to break-up—you or the other person?

12. Describe how the break-up happened: what did you or the other person say or do to end it?

13. Did you feel depressed, sad or angry, or did you feel free, liberated? If you were upset, how did you get over it? Did you feel stupid for feeling hurt? Do you still want the person back?

14. Did you express your anger, outrage or hurt by taking revenge? How? If, did you tell your lover his/her actions were unfair?

15. What is the most emotionally violent thing a lover has ever done to you?

Sexual Politics in Relationships

16. Do you feel you and your lover are friends? Enemies? Co-existing? Emotionally attuned? In touch?

17. Can you talk about anything and everything? Or does your partner become silent and irritable if you are not careful?

18. Are there a lot of silences in the relationship? What kind? Are they a problem?

19. When are you happiest in the relationship? What makes you angriest?

20. During arguments, do you often feel the other person has the upper hand? If so, how does this happen?

21. What level of emotional withholding, if any, is going on? On whose part?

22. Do you often wonder how your lover feels about you, or does s/he make it clear, so you don't have to wonder?

23. Does your partner listen and really hear you when you are trying to explain something? When you are upset? How does s/he respond?

24. How often do you feel that the other person is refusing to acknowledge what you are saying during an argument, or twisting your meaning to avoid responding to your point?

25. Does your partner use clichés to address you, such as "Calm down, dear, and you'll feel better," or "Maybe you shouldn't think about it so much"? Do you use clichés in return?

26. Do you shout or cry during arguments? Why? What is the usual scenario during a conflict? Are your remarks met with silence and ridicule, or do positive conversations ensue?

27. Do you often feel you are doing the emotional housework in the relationship—bringing up misunderstandings that might cause resentment, finding out how the other person is feeling in order to keep channels of communication open, and so on? Or is your partner doing it too?

28. Did you ever enter therapy to try to solve personal problems related to a relationship? Did it help?

29. Have you ever loved someone who hurt you deeply, in spite of what had happened, in spite of your desire not to love them any longer—indeed, in spite of your common sense that they were "no good" for you?

30. What did you think about yourself in this situation? Did you have anyone to talk to? Did you think you were "picking the wrong men"?

31. Do or did you take pills or tranquilizers? To sleep? Alcohol? When did you begin? Why?

32. Is there such a thing as a New Man?

33. In the past twenty years, have men's attitudes to women changed—dramatically, quite a lot, not enough, hardly at all, or for the worse?

Being Single: Sex and the Double Standard

34. If you are single, do you like being on your own?

35. Do you date a lot, relatively infrequently—or not at all?

36. Is it easy to meet someone you like, are attracted to, and respect?

37. Is it a form of power to be "young and beautiful," or "young and sexy"? Why or why not?

38. Does a woman get more social prestige being single or being married? Would you rather be married?

39. Do you think most single men today want to be married? Or do you think they are afraid of it and want to avoid commitments, being "tied down" to even a steady dating relationship? Do men you know talk about needing to be "free"?

40. Have you had any "one-night stands"? That is, sex with someone just one time? How did you feel about this? Was this your idea or theirs?

41. If it was not your idea, did the man tell you beforehand, that he just wanted to have sex and might never call you again? Did he give you the impression of not being "like that," of being "more serious"? What did he say or do before sex?

42. What did he say after? When did you discover his real (or lack of) feelings? Or did you express hurt or anger? What did he say?

43. Have you ever been called a "slut," "tramp," "bitch" or "whore"? By whom? (someone you knew, or a stranger?) What were your feelings? How did you respond? Did it depress you, or make you self-conscious?

44. Do you admire Madonna? Do you admire Mother Teresa? Why? What do they stand for, to you?

45. Which one, if either, would you like to be more like?

46. For whom has the greater "sexual freedom" of the past twenty years been a positive change? Women, men, both or neither?

47. Has your sexual life changed because of AIDS? With a regular partner? With a new partner? Do you carry condoms?

48. Do you think women have sexual freedom today? What does the phrase "sexual freedom" mean?

49. What would you like women's sexual freedom to mean?

Sexuality

50. Are you satisfied with your sex life? Would you rather have sex or a great dinner out?

51. What is the best part of sex for you?

52. Do you ever have sex when you think it is a bore? How often?

53. Do you like to hear "I love you" during sex? Do you like to say it?

54. Is it easy for you to have orgasms? By yourself? With a partner?

55. What is the easiest way for you to orgasm? Through masturbation, clitoral stimulation by hand from a partner, oral sex, intercourse (coitus), or with a vibrator?

56. If you orgasm during coitus, where are you getting the most intense stimulation, that is, the stimulation that actually makes

you orgasm? By added clitoral stimulation from your partner, or by your own clitoral stimulation (masturbation) during intercourse? By being on top and rubbing against him? By friction of the penis inside the vagina, without other stimulation?

57. When you had your first orgasm with another person, which activity was it during?

58. Did you first discover masturbation on your own, or did you read about it? How old were you? Did your parents know about it? Friends?

59. Have you ever masturbated with a partner? During intercourse? During general caresses? Was it hard to do the first time? How did you feel? What was his/her reaction?

60. When you masturbate to orgasm, do you have your legs together or apart? Which way is it easier for you to orgasm?

61. How often do you masturbate? How many orgasms do you usually have? How many orgasms do you usually have with a partner?

62. Do you like exploring a man's body? His penis and testicles? Anus and buttocks? Have you ever penetrated a man's anus with your finger? How did you feel about this?

63. How do you feel about giving a man oral sex? That is, going down on your lover? Is it an act of love, and does it turn you on— or do you feel used and pressured?

64. Do you like, or would you like to try, exploring a woman's body? Her breasts? Her clitoris? Her vagina? Anus and buttocks? How do you feel about giving her oral sex? Do you like the taste and smell? Do most women like you to do this, or feel shy and uncomfortable?

65. Do you like for oral sex to be done to you? What do you think about how you look and smell? (How about during menstruation?) Do you feel uncomfortable asking your lover for oral sex? Do you orgasm this way?

66. Can your partner stimulate you with his/her fingers on your clitoris to orgasm?

67. Have you shown someone how to masturbate you—that is, how to stimulate you to orgasm with their hand? Do most men offer you clitoral stimulation by hand or mouth for orgasm, without being asked?

68. Do you like to be stimulated or penetrated anally? By a finger? Penis? Dildo? How?

69. Do you like to be stimulated vaginally? How?

70. Do you ever fake orgasms during sex? When?

71. Do you feel pressured into sex sometimes? Into liking sex?

Wanting it? Into liking certain activities during sex? How are you pressured—to prove you are loving? To be "hip"?

72. How would you like to change sex?

73. Do you use fantasies to help you orgasm? Which ones? During sex with a partner? During masturbation? What do you think about?

74. Do you like rough sex? What do you think of bondage-discipline? Spanking? Sadomasochism? Have you ever experienced them? Fantasized about them? Had rape fantasies? Been tied up? What were the fantasies about?

75. What do you think of pornography? Do you look at it? How did you feel when you first saw it? What does pornography imply about what it means to be a woman?

76. Do you mind if (your) children see pornographic depictions of sexuality in popular magazines and on newsstands?

77. Do you think sexual art or pornography should be banned? Do you think pornography is anti-woman, increases violence and disrespect to women?

78. Have you ever been forced into sex, or raped? Whom did you tell? How did you feel? How important was this experience to you?

79. Do you think it would be possible to have a society in which sexuality did not have this darker side? Do you think it is "natural" for men to rape women?

80. Why do you think the word "fuck" has come to be a swear word, as in "Fuck you"? Why is the cultural connotation of intercourse (coitus) that the man is "doing something to" the woman ("fucking her")?

81. Do you ever find yourself having to make a conscious effort during sex not to think of it that way, not to think of yourself as being "fucked"? Does this phrase give sex dirty connotations to you, i.e., anyone who gets "fucked" must be slightly "bitchy," or somewhat of a "slut"?

82. Do you ever feel you have to hold back during sex, not be too "wild" or carried away, for fear that the man may think you are something of a "slut" or a "whore"? If he thought that, would that create problems?

83. When were you the most sexually free or carried away with a man, and how did you enjoy it? How did he react? During sex? Later?

84. Do you think men know how to have fun in bed?

Relationships with Women/Growing Up Female

85. What is or has been your most important relationship with a woman in your life? Describe the woman you have loved the most, the woman you have hated the most.

86. What do you like about your closest woman friend? What do you do together? When do you see each other? How do you feel when you are together—do you have a good time? What does she do that you like least?

87. Are women a primary source of affection in your life? Physically? Emotionally?

88. Were you or are you close to your mother? Did she work outside the home, or was she a full-time mother and homemaker? Did you like her? Admire her? How did you feel about her style of dressing? Are you like her?

89. As a child, were you closer to your mother or to your father? What did you like most and least about them?

90. Was your mother affectionate with you? Did she speak sweetly to you? Sing to you? Bathe you and do your hair? What were the clashes between you? When was she angriest? What do you think of her today? Do you like to spend time with her?

91. Was your father affectionate? How? Did you talk? Go places together? Did you like him? Fear him? Respect him? What did you argue about? What do you think of him today?

92. Were your parents affectionate together in front of you? Did they argue? What did you learn from your father was the proper attitude toward your mother? What did you learn from your mother was the proper attitude toward your father?

93. Did your mother show you how to be "feminine," special ways to act like a girl or a "lady"? How would you define "femininity"? Do you like it? What about "masculinity"?

94. Were you a "tomboy"? Was it fun? Were you warned against playing "boys" games, acting "unladylike"? Were you urged to be a "good girl"? Were you rebellious?

95. Do you have a daughter? How do you feel about her? Have you talked to her about menstruation and sexuality? What did you say? What did she say?

96. Do you have a son? Who has explained to him about sexuality and pregnancy? Does he look at pornography? Are you worried about the influence of sexual violence on television and in street corner magazines on him? Can you and he talk about these subjects?

97. What things about women in general do you admire? What are women's best qualities, and what keeps women from attaining

equal political power with men? Why don't women find candidates to represent their issues and vote for them?

98. What do you think about the women's movement? Do you consider yourself a feminist, or in favor of the women's movement?

99. What do you think is the position of older women in our society? How do you feel about getting older? Who are the women with the most power in today's world?

100. Have you talked with your mother, sister or daughters—or your best friend—about your sexuality? Do they know if you masturbate? Have you told them you don't orgasm from intercourse (if you don't)? Have you explained your sexuality in any detail to them? Do you know about theirs? Would you like to?

101. Do you enjoy being a woman? What about it would you never give up, no matter what?

THANK YOU!

Send your answers to:
Shere Hite, P.O. Box 5282, F.D.R. Station, New York, New York, 10022.